YOU CAN

Motivate reluctant readers

Kate Ruttle

FOR AGES
4-7

"Reluctant readers can sometimes read very well but are not motivated..."
('Reading for Purpose and Pleasure', Ofsted)

Credits

Author
Kate Ruttle

Development Editor
Kate Pedlar

Project Editor
Fabia Lewis

Series Designer
Catherine Perera

Cover Designer
Anna Oliwa

Cover photography
© Blend Images/Punchstock

Design
Q2A Media

Text © 2009, Kate Ruttle
© 2009, Scholastic Ltd

Designed using Adobe InDesign

Published by Scholastic Ltd
Villiers House
Clarendon Avenue
Leamington Spa
Warwickshire CV32 5PR

www.scholastic.co.uk

Printed by Bell and Bain Ltd.
1 2 3 4 5 6 7 8 9   9 0 1 2 3 4 5 6 7 8

British Library Cataloguing-in-Publication Data
A catalogue record for this book is available from the British Library.
ISBN 978-1407-10173-6

The right of Kate Ruttle to be identified as the author of this work has been asserted by her in accordance with the Copyright, Designs and Patents Act 1988.

Due to the nature of the web, the publisher cannot guarantee the content or links of any of the websites referred to. All links were checked June 2008, but It is the responsibility of the reader to assess the suitability of websites and check that links are still live.

Every effort has been made to trace copyright holders for the works reproduced in this book, and the publishers apologise for any inadvertent omissions.

Contents

Introduction 5

**Chapter 1 You can... identify obstacles
to reading** **6**
You can... Explore reasons for reluctance to read **6**
You can... Explore possible reading difficulties **7**

Chapter 2 You can... tackle difficulties in reading . . **8**
You can... Ensure phonic strategies. **8**
You can... Teach word structure **9**
You can... Teach reading for meaning **10**
You can... Teach punctuation **11**
You can... Make your classroom dyslexia friendly **12**

Chapter 3 You can... read without books **13**
You can... Read from patterns **13**
You can... Read from puzzles **14**
You can... Read from pictures. **15**
You can... Read from comic strips. **16**

Chapter 4 You can... read from the screen **17**
You can... Read from TV. **17**
You can... Read from film. **18**
You can... Read using computer games **19**
You can... Read for information on-line **20**

**Chapter 5 You can... teach reading
comprehension** **21**
You can... Sequence pictures **21**
You can... Encourage creative responses to stories **22**
You can... Match text to pictures **23**
You can... Find the main idea. **24**
You can... Explore what's *not* been said **25**

Chapter 6 You can... enjoy reading poetry **26**
You can... Read poetry together. **26**
You can... Play with rhyme. **27**
You can... Recognise rhythm and beat **28**
You can... Read line by line. **29**
You can... Hold your own poetry award **30**

Chapter 7 You can... enjoy sharing stories **31**
You can... Create a story world. **31**
You can... Write exciting snippets. **32**
You can... Select books to read aloud. **33**
You can... Find out about authors and illustrators. **34**
You can... Invite an author or illustrator into school **35**

Contents

Chapter 8 You can... enjoy reading for information **36**
You can... Read environmental print **36**
You can... Make an information tool kit **37**
You can... Use computers **38**
You can... Teach children how to follow instructions **39**
You can... Visit a library **40**

Chapter 9 You can... give reasons for reading in school **41**
You can... Find out about reading habits **41**
You can... Set up treasure hunts **42**
You can... Use your role-play corner **43**
You can... Set up a book quiz **44**
You can... Use your school website **45**
You can... Read together at 2.30 on Thursday **46**

Chapter 10 You can... encourage reading at home **47**
You can... Get involved in the Summer Reading Challenge **47**
You can... Help parents to read with their children **48**
You can... Use ideas from the National Literacy Trust **49**
You can... Encourage RIBIT **50**
You can... Support the Six Book Challenge **51**

Chapter 11 You can... set targets for improvement **52**
You can... Agree targets for improvement with children **52**
You can... Use targets for improvement **53**
You can... Choose activities to reach your targets **54**
You can... Evaluate an intervention **55**

Photocopiables **56**
Child's profile **56**
Phonological awareness MOT **57**
Behaviours associated with dyslexia **58**
Getting ready to read – booklet pages 1 and 4 . . . . **59**
Getting ready to read – booklet pages 2 and 3 . . . . **60**
Becoming a reader – booklet pages 1 and 4 . . . . **61**
Becoming a reader – booklet pages 2 and 3 . . . . **62**

Index **63**

Introduction

This book aims to support you in encouraging your young reluctant readers to engage with learning to read. As Foundation Stage and Key Stage 1 teachers, you share the enjoyment of opening the door to reading with your children and it can be disheartening when some of them don't follow you through. Disheartening for you, but potentially so much more damaging for the child. Reading is by far the most important skill that you teach children in their first years of school, and those who are unable to engage may well suffer throughout formal schooling. So the challenge is: how do we engage them?

Identifying the barriers to learning

The first task is to identify the barriers: is there a problem with attitude, with sight, with learning, with experience, with maturity...? This book will help you to establish what the problems may be through suggesting simple questions you can ask and by providing some classroom screening procedures. Thereafter, the book falls roughly into two parts.

Teaching skills for reading

If attitude is a problem, many reading skills can be taught in exciting ways, without books. While you immerse children in a variety of stories, you can improve the likelihood of their feeling like successful readers by developing their skill base through non-book based activities, including reading comics and pictures, using jigsaws and sequencing cards, and by using computers or exploiting their interest in TV programmes.

Practising skills for reading

In Key Stage 1, many of the children who *can* read, as well as those who *could* read if they chose to make the effort, will do better if they have clear, exciting reasons for reading. Research by the National Literacy Trust also suggests that many boys respond better when there is a level of competition. So, reading in order to select a winner for school-based book awards; reading because someone has asked you to find the answer; reading to solve the clues in a treasure hunt... all of these ideas give children reasons to read.

Throughout this book you will find ideas: some of which will be familiar or a twist on a familiar idea, and some of which will probably be new to you. The ideas have been tried and tested in Foundation Stage and Key Stage 1 classrooms and all have been used to engage reluctant readers. Use them, adapt them and develop from them strategies and activities that will work in your classroom and will help to ensure that you can motivate your reluctant readers.

You Can... **Explore reasons for reluctance to read**

Before you can help your 'reluctant readers' it is important to try to unpick the reasons why they are reluctant, because different problems will require different solutions. You may well have more than one reluctant reader in your class and if this is the case, it will be useful to think about them individually while you consider how best to help them.

Thinking points

● What is it about a child's behaviour that makes you think of them as a 'reluctant reader'? Is the child happy to engage in the curriculum until they burst into tears when asked to read? Is this a child who is doing well in maths but making poor progress in reading? Does the child always hide their reading record so you can't check it, or mess around when they are supposed to be completing a phonics worksheet?

● There are many possible reasons why a child may be reluctant to read: their experiences of reading at home; their pre-school awareness of books; their own self-perception; their interest in reading or their overall maturity. Alternatively, reluctance may be the result of a reading difficulty. Whatever the reason, it is important to do some detective work to uncover the reason for a reluctance to read.

Tips, ideas and activities

As part of your exploration into why a child is a reluctant reader, it may be useful to:

● Talk to parents/carers and to other members of staff to find out if there is any history of reading problems in the family. If so, what can you discover about these problems?

● Check whether there is a problem around processing language. This is not an uncommon problem among learners in the early stages of language acquisition. If children's language processing skills are poor, then their ability to understand text will be affected and this may impact on their motivation and interest.

● Find out about the child's own interests. Is it possible that the child hasn't yet been motivated to read because they've never come across a text that has 'spoken' to them? Present as wide a variety of books as possible, including comics, TV-related books, puzzle books, catalogues, interactive books and so on, to discover which kind of reading matter grabs the child's interest.

● Watch the child's reactions when you read aloud. Does the child listen attentively – or at least listen? Can they talk about stories, participate in related drama and role play, express opinions, sequence events? Or does the lack of interest in reading extend to include stories?

● Try to interest the child in non-fiction books. Many children – boys in particular – are more interested in non-fiction than in stories. There are many excellent non-fiction books available as part of reading schemes, so if a child is interested in non-fiction rather than fiction this no longer needs to stand in the way of their progress in reading.

You Can... **Explore possible reading difficulties**

It is always worth questioning whether an apparent reluctance to read is masking a reading difficulty. Even very young children can hide a difficulty with distracting behaviours in order to focus attention on something that they can control (the behaviour) rather than something over which they have no control (the reading difficulty). Not all reluctant readers have reading difficulties, but some of them do.

Thinking points

● What is your attitude (and that of your school and local authority) to diagnosing reading difficulties in young children? Some people are vehemently against early diagnosis, arguing that many problems will rectify themselves if children are given appropriate support and are allowed to develop at their own pace, without pressure. Others argue that early intervention is crucial in order to minimise disruption to a child's education.

● Part of the problem with early diagnosis is that young children develop at vastly different rates. Labelling a child as having reading difficulties too soon may make them self-conscious about reading and alert them to how difficult it is. On the other hand, allowing children to move through school as non-readers will inevitably lead to problems of low self-esteem and self-belief.

Tips, ideas and activities

● The ideas in this book will offer you guidance on the signs to look for if you think a child has a reading difficulty.

● As part of your own exploration into the likelihood of there being a reading difficulty, use the photocopiable 'Child's profile' on page 56 to keep a regular record of the child's progress while, at the same time, you try to find out more about the child's development.

● Begin with the easy things: has the child had a recent vision and hearing test? If so, what were the results? Has the child ever been referred to a speech and language therapist?

● Compare the progress the child is making in reading with that made in the rest of the curriculum. In particular, what are their fine and gross motor skills like? How well developed is the vocabulary for maths? Does the child understand the concepts of time such as *before*, *after*, *first*, or the language of length such as *longer*, *shorter* and so on?

● If the child appears to have problems across the curriculum you will need to consider whether this is due to maturity, to social and domestic issues or to other problems. If there are no obvious reasons for the child's global lack of attainment, you may want to refer to your SENCO for further advice.

● If you think that the problems are specific to reading and writing, try the photocopiable sheet 'Phonological awareness MOT' on page 57.

● Whether or not you request additional help for the child, you will need to continue to promote learning. Use results of your assessment – together with ideas in this book – to develop reading skills as far as you can, without putting undue stress on the child.

You Can... **Ensure phonic strategies**

After the Rose Report (2006) the consensus is that phonics is critical in the early development of reading. The Rose Report concluded that teaching children to use a number of strategies simultaneously is likely to be confusing, rather than supportive, during early attempts at reading. So phonics is the only strategy we should now be teaching in these early stages. Children are likely to struggle with reading if their phonological awareness is limited. It's worth doing a quick phonics MOT to check that there isn't a problem.

Thinking points

● Research since the mid-1980s has developed the understanding that phonological awareness is the most reliable indicator of future success in reading. Phase 1 of the synthetic phonics scheme *Letters and Sounds* (DfES, 2007) supports the development of crucial phonological skills. Although children in Reception and KS1 are meant to be working beyond this phase, continue to ensure that the Phase 1 activities and skills are consolidated orally: rushing forwards at this stage is likely to cause difficulties before children have made sufficient progress.

Tips, ideas and activities

A phonological awareness MOT can include the following activity types, all of which should be supported by pictures or objects to ensure that memory isn't impeding phonological processing.

● Check that children can orally segment a word into phonemes, for example, *cat, c-a-t.*

● Ask children to tell you what the new word would be if you:
  ● Changed the initial letter.
  ● Changed the final letter.
  ● Changed the middle sound in a short vowel CVC word.

● Can children tell you what the new word would be if you changed letters in a CVC word? Do this activity orally, without written words. For example, say *cat. Change the c to p* and the children say the new word.

● Show the children pictures and ask them to tell you if pairs of words rhyme:
  ● Use words which don't rhyme for example, *cat, dog.*
  ● Use words that nearly rhyme for example, *cat, cap.*

● Ask children to give you a string of rhyming words (which can include non-words).

● Can children tell you the odd one out from three or four words? Ask questions like:
  ● *Which one begins with a different sound?*
  ● *Which one doesn't rhyme?*
  ● *Which one has a different end sound?*
  ● *Which one has a different middle sound?*

Use the photocopiable sheet 'Phonological awareness MOT' on page 57 to keep a record of progress.

You Can... **Teach word structure**

Many children struggle with reading once they move away from easily decodable texts and begin to meet tricky words. At this stage, the tricky words are likely to fall into one of four categories: high-frequency words, words with long vowel phonemes (particularly those with split digraphs, such as, 'a-e'), words with more than one syllable and words with common suffixes. Teaching children strategies for tackling these tricky words will dramatically increase their reading success, confidence and motivation.

Thinking points

● Before you begin to teach word structure, it's worth checking that the children haven't missed any important teaching points before they reached your class. Children who have missed the 'phonics bus' in earlier years (perhaps due to absence, glue ear, immature hearing, or an inability to sit and focus) will need additional opportunities to learn and recognise common digraphs, otherwise you'll leave these children standing at an earlier bus stop and they'll always struggle to catch up.

Tips, ideas and activities

High-frequency words:

● The recommendation in *Letters and Sounds* is that children are taught to tackle the reading of high-frequency words by looking for what they know and using that to scaffold their blending of the word. As children progress through Phase 5 of *Letters and Sounds* they will develop an awareness that the same written grapheme can have different pronunciations (for example, the *ow* in *now* and *blow*).

● As you teach new phonics, revisit any words that were previously tricky words but which are now decodable.

● Teach children to scan unknown words for letter patterns. If they are still trying to blend *rain* as *r-a-i-n*:
  ○ Use phoneme frames, sound buttons and highlighter pens to emphasise letter patterns.
  ○ Give them word-building activities using plastic letters and computer programs which show the digraph already joined as one unit.

● Many children feel intimidated when they see a polysyllabic word so they read the first letter and then guess or give up. In order that they can move on with their reading, they need to be willing to try to tackle these words.

● Check that they understand the idea of a syllable. Clap out the syllable structure of names or rhymes. Secure rhythm through music activities.

● Carry out sorting activities so that children put words containing different numbers of syllables into different sets. (Try using animal names for this.)

● Introduce compound words, helping children to understand that they should look out for whole words within words and then read these one at a time.

You Can... **Teach reading for meaning**

From the beginning, it is important for children to understand that reading is about making meaning and communication. As children develop awareness of environmental print and then begin to decode phonically regular texts, it is important to remind them to check that what they are reading makes sense: too many uncorrected and unrecognised errors are made by children 'barking at print', with no expectation of it making any sense. The clearest clues that children are reading for meaning come when they self-correct errors.

Thinking points
● What kinds of environmental print do you have in your classroom to encourage children to make meaning as they read? Signs reminding them to wash their hands, telling them how many children can play in the sand, or where to find classroom equipment can be used as active teaching points for making meaning when reading.

● Read the signs with the children and then ask them to read the signs back to you.

● Change the locations of classroom equipment every few weeks, for example, change the order of trays in a storage unit and then talk to the children about how they can find the equipment.

Tips, ideas and activities
● When you listen to children reading, insist on the reading making sense. Inaccuracies which keep the sense when reading can be allowed; those that lose the meaning should be corrected before moving on to the next page or finishing the book.

● Let children ask you questions about their books. Model finding the answers in the pictures and the text.

● Encourage role play based around the stories in their reading books. Let them refer to the books for ideas.

● Work with the children to make games based on the books. Make simple track games where you move on and miss turns according to events that happen in the text.

● Use story books as the basis for sequencing activities: try retelling the story or role playing events using small world characters or puppets and record scenes using a digital or video camera; make zigzag books showing the main events in a reading book.

● Write simple decodable texts yourself – the children are unlikely to read them critically and will be so impressed that you wrote them. Ask children to draw the illustrations: if a child can illustrate a story they have read independently, then they are making meaning.

● Once children are able to answer questions based on pictures, introduce similar questions based on shared reading of texts. As you do so, show children where in the text or pictures you are able to find the answers to the questions.

● Ask children simple questions when they are reading. Encourage them to look back at the text for answers.

You Can... **Teach punctuation**

Can your children use the word 'sentence'? Do they know what one is? Ask them to define 'a sentence'. They are likely to know that sentences have capital letters and full stops, but do they know that putting a full stop after a collection of words doesn't mean that they make a sentence? Encourage them to explore the idea of sentence until you have a definition which involves the fact that it must make sense.

Thinking points

● The prior learning around sentences for Year 1 unit 1 (Narrative) is that children should be able to '...begin to form a simple sentence when attempting writing...'. By the end of this unit, children are being asked to write three sentences. By the end of Year 2, children should be writing in a sustained form in narrative, using simple and compound sentences and maintaining a consistent tense. By the end of Year 2, they are also reading well enough to discuss events and characters. This implies a substantial development in the children's understanding of what makes a sentence.

● Is a better understanding of what makes a sentence something that evolves naturally, or is this something that you need to teach? If it comes naturally, why do so many children fail to mark sentences with full stops in their writing or read without taking note of punctuation?

Tips, ideas and activities

● Have discussions around the idea of 'sentence' with your children. *What do they know about sentences?* Collect their information and agree on a class definition. (For example: *A sentence begins with a capital letter, ends with punctuation and makes sense by itself.*) As you do shared reading, compare sentences from texts against the class definition. Does the definition hold up, or does it need to be tweaked?

● Over time, add some desirable attributes of a good sentence to the class definition, for example, *It has some description*; *some have words like* and, but, then, because...

● Check that the children understand that statements, questions and exclamations are all types of sentences, each with their own 'end-of-sentence' punctuation.

● Ask children to collect 'super' sentences from their reading, and select your own examples of super sentences from the children's writing. Make a display, or a book, of these sentences so that children can read them.

● Add good sentences to wordbanks to support children's writing.

● Let the children make 'human sentences'. Give each child, in a group, a word and ask them to organise themselves into a sentence. Remind them to use clues, such as the capital letter and the full stop, to identify the first and last words. Can they put all the other words in the right order?

● Occasionally, keep one of the words back, or add in an extra word, so that the children can't make a proper sentence using all of the words. Refer to your class definition of a sentence to judge whether or not the children's reason for not using all of the words to make a sentence is a good one.

● Use computer programs that enable you to display sentences with scrambled words. Remind children to add punctuation once they have unscrambled the words.

You Can... # Make your classroom dyslexia friendly

The British Dyslexia Association estimates that ten per cent of the population is dyslexic, with approximately four per cent being sufficiently dyslexic for it to cause reading and writing problems. Poor short-term memory, together with poor phonological awareness, is a key indicator of dyslexia. Dyslexic children find sequencing activities difficult and often have poor organisational skills. If you are concerned, it may be worth asking your SENCO to arrange a dyslexia screen, although some authorities don't like to screen children who are under the age of seven.

Thinking points

● Under the Disability Discrimination Act (2005) dyslexia is classed as a disability since its impact on a child is *'...a physical or mental impairment which has a substantial and long-term adverse effect on his or her ability to carry out normal day-to-day activities.'*

● Dyslexia cannot be 'cured' although people with dyslexia can successfully be taught strategies for coping with, and overcoming, its impact on their daily life. On its own, dyslexia is rarely severe enough to stop a child from reaching their educational potential as long as the disability is recognised and catered for.

Tips, ideas and activities

Whether or not a child has a diagnosis of dyslexia, there are ways you can make it easier for all children to learn to read:

● Use as many multi-sensory techniques as possible when you are teaching.

● Use colour when you are writing on a board. If you make each line of text a different colour, children will have a better chance of finding their place after resting their eyes.

● Check that the glare of an interactive whiteboard isn't inhibiting reading.

● Can children can see better when you photocopy their work onto off-white paper or allow them to read through a piece of coloured acetate? If so, you may want to refer them for an Irlens test for scopic sensitivity. For more information visit the following website: www.irlen.org.uk

● Make sure that important concepts like common graphemes and high-frequency words are 'overlearned' so that children know them automatically, without thinking.

● Provide lots of opportunities for recognising graphemes and words in different context.
   ● Give daily opportunities for recognising them at speed. Make a 'word wall' or a 'grapheme wall' on which you write graphemes or words. Time the children to see how many words/ graphemes they can read in 30 seconds or one minute. Repeat for a week.

● The photocopiable sheet 'Behaviours associated with dyslexia' on page 58 gives you some signs to look out for, although this should not be used as a diagnostic test: always seek advice from your SENCO if you think a child in your class may be dyslexic.

You Can... **Read from patterns**

Proficiency in reading is dependent on proficiency in recognising patterns and distinguishing detail. Patterns can be oral, visual, temporal or even tactile; they can involve matching or sequencing; they can also involve sounds, events, objects, colours, numbers or letters; they can be identified in the environment, in books, on paper, in classrooms... patterns are all around us. If children are reluctant to read from books, many early reading skills can be taught and reinforced, away from the page, using patterns.

Thinking points

● If children's reluctance to engage with reading stems from fear of failure, from being uninterested in the idea of reading, from finding it hard to sit still or from a myriad of other reasons, it's important to focus on developing critical skills for reading, even if the child won't look at a book.

● For children who aren't yet 'ready' to learn to read, you can increase their likely success through pattern-making activities, as patterns are involved at every level of reading.

Tips, ideas and activities

● Develop the games and activities suggested in Phase 1 of *Letters and Sounds*. The recommendation is that this phase is initiated pre-school but most Reception aged children will continue to benefit from these activities for the entire Reception year while they are learning the phonemes and graphemes within phases 2 and 3.

● Focus particularly on rhyme. Play games such as rhyming lotto and rhyming *I spy*; generate strings of rhyming words – including some non-words; read and recite finger rhymes, number rhymes and nursery rhymes.

● Buy or draw pictures of adapted nursery rhymes such as:
Humpty Dumpty sat on a box/chair/rug,
Humpty Dumpty saw a…
Humpty Dumpty went on a bus/train/lorry,
Humpty Dumpty saw…
Use the nursery rhymes to play rhyming words as well as to check that children know the originals.

● Let children collect and display pictures representing words that begin with the same sound as their name.

● Take photographs of 'before' and 'after' events in the classroom. Build up to taking up to four or five photographs. Ask children to sequence them, to explain the events and tell the story. Establish the idea that there is a sequence of events.

● Use puppets to retell familiar stories. Take photographs of the puppets. Ask children to sequence the photographs and retell the story. Check that the children are able to link events orally. Children who struggle to read, even at this stage, tend to describe individual pictures without acknowledging the fact that the pictures are related to each other.

You Can... **Read from puzzles**

Talk to your reluctant readers about what they do at home. Many of them are likely to spend some of their time playing computer games. If you can find out about the games they play, either from them or from the internet, you will learn more about the kinds of puzzles they are used to solving: most computer games involve some sort of puzzle. Once you know about the puzzles the children are used to solving in their own time, you can use this information to set them puzzle challenges in school.

Thinking points

● What kinds of puzzle activities do children have access to, in your class? The attitude you display towards puzzles will impact on the children's willingness to do them.

● In the early stages, reading is something of a multi-layered puzzle for children. Using phonics to work out a word involves first recognising the graphemes, then remembering all the sounds in the right sequence before trying to blend these together to make a sensible sounding word. If this level of puzzle is too challenging for children, we can try to break it down and teach them each of the important puzzle-solving skills, separately.

Tips, ideas and activities

● Make solving puzzles something 'cool' and admirable in the context of your classroom.

● Give jigsaw puzzles to children throughout the day, not just as a low status wet-play activity.

● Making numeracy into puzzles is really easy: turn number sentences into word problems. Challenge the children to make up their own word puzzle to solve a number sentence: for example, if they know that $25 + 3 = 28$, they can suggest a puzzle story that goes: *a wasp stung 25 people before dinner. After dinner it was sleepy, so it only stung another 3. How many people did it sting altogether?*

● Give children practice at 'spot the odd one out' and 'spot the difference' puzzles. These are easily found on the internet where you can select those that are at an appropriate level of challenge for your class. You could also ask children to bring in their comics and look at the puzzle pages within them. If possible, cut out and laminate the puzzles for future use.

● Let the children be detectives. Hide clues (for example, letters or numbers) around the school or classroom and take photos of the places where you hid the clues. Let the children follow the photos, in sequence, to collect your clues and use them to solve a puzzle (for example, a word or a number sentence).

● Use games to stimulate memory, particularly those which need you to remember a sequence. The traditional 'pairs' memory game is a good place to start, but also try variations on 'Kim's game'. Put a number of objects on a tray in a line and then remove one for the children to spot, or ask the children to remember all the objects that have been removed, in order. Oral games like 'I went shopping and I bought…' are useful for this purpose, as are games using cumulative rhythms in music lessons.

You Can... **Read from pictures**

Pictures are a non-threatening way into reading for many children. By the time they are aware that they don't or can't read, children often feel inadequate and they can develop an attitude of: 'I'll fail so I won't even try'. For these children in particular, pictures can be very important in drawing children back into books. Allow the children to spend time with you, on a one-to-one basis, talking about the pictures in a high quality and age-appropriate picture book. You can read the words, but you should ask the child to read the pictures.

Thinking points

● What turns young children into reluctant readers? If they struggle with words, you can give them additional teaching in phonics and word recognition. But, there are still some children who can decode and recognise words, yet who show no interest in reading. For these children, pictures can be a vital motivator to read.

● When you think of reading with pictures, you need to think beyond pictures in picture books: there are pictures in non-fiction books; there are pictures in art galleries, in newspapers, in advertisements, on TV and computer screens. Children are often brought up in a very visual world, but they don't often take time to consider the pictures around them. Developing 'visual literacy' is an important skill for children living in the 21st century, as well as for reading.

Tips, ideas and activities

● Use pictures to develop children's comprehension skills. As you talk about a picture, distinguish between three types of discussion:

   ○ *It's there*: this type of discussion raises questions which relate directly to objects or people in the pictures. These questions relate to direct-evidence questions in reading comprehension.

   ○ *Work it out*: this type of discussion raises questions, the answers to which are not directly in the picture, but for which we can use clues to deduce a hypothesis. For example, the way that backgrounds are drawn may help children to infer whether a character is tidy or messy.

   ○ *What do you think?* This question develops inferential skills as it asks children to focus on aspects of the picture where the artist is trying to create something other than what the picture shows. For example, the artist's use of colour, or the way in which someone is standing may let us know how they are feeling.

If children can develop their comprehension skills through looking at pictures, they can often transfer these skills to reading. This makes reading more interesting and may help reluctant readers to try to engage more willingly.

● Let reluctant readers spend time looking at pictures in non-fiction books. In these books, the captions under the pictures are often readable once children have 'read' and understood the image. The images in non-fiction books are often designed to attract the eye of a young reader and there are many titles that appeal to young children.

● Encourage children to draw pictures themselves. For example, write a book with a simple text that is phonically constructed or written around the interests of the children, and then allow them to illustrate the book. Give them time to do high quality illustrations in order to show that you value the pictures as much as the text.

You Can... **Read from comic strips**

Comics can be very motivating reads, particularly for your lower attaining and reluctant readers. Comics for children of this age generally have very strong characters, often with a TV tie-in, so the reader immediately understands something about what is happening in the story. The nature of the comic strip also means that a visually literate child can work out what's going on in the pictures without feeling threatened by the text. Using comic strips as part of a rich and varied selection of texts is a way of showing how much you value all different kinds of reading experience.

Thinking points

● Comics aimed at children of this age tend to fall into one of two camps: they are either educational comics which tend to have comic strips with blocks of text under each image or they are cartoon tie-ins, often imported from America, with more conventional comic strips where the story is told through the pictures and dialogue. Which kind is going to prove more useful for the children in your class? Are you able to justify to the children why you have selected one type or the other, or will you ensure that both types of comic are available for use in your class?

● It is useful to find out more about the characters and stories in a comic before investing in it as a classroom resource. Is the children's perception that some characters 'only fight', or are there other characteristics which you can build on?

Tips, ideas and activities

● Find out what the children know about comics, particularly in respect of the characters from the comics you have selected. What are their perceptions about reading comics? Do they value them or believe them to be worthless? Talk about strategies for making meaning from comics: what are the children able to do?

● If you are using a comic strip with dialogue, ask children first to talk their way through what they think is happening in the story. Give them guidance if they are wrong in their interpretation. This prior knowledge will be critical in helping the child to read some of the dialogue.

● Treat the comic strip as if it were a playscript, with different characters speaking. Take the trickiest and longest part for yourself. Work as a group to read the comic strip. Encourage the group to give each other as much support as necessary. Be aware of the errors the children make, but also look for the strategies that enable them to read tricky words. They often tackle harder words within a comic strip than in a book.

● Use all parts of a comic, including the puzzle pages. Most of the activities in the comic will involve reading to some extent. Reading instructions so you know how to solve a puzzle helps to reinforce the value of reading.

● If you cut out some of the pictures in a familiar comic strip, can the children re-sequence them? Discuss the strategies they use to work out the sequence.

● Try to build up a selection of well-preserved comics for a reading display table. Many children who are otherwise reluctant to read will spend time sitting with a friend and talking over the adventures of a favourite TV character who features in a comic.

You Can... **Read from TV**

Children's reading from a TV screen is often superior to that from a book. Many children also have TV tie-in books and comics. These artefacts can be very useful as a way of persuading reluctant children to take an interest in reading. If you are willing to develop ideas from TV programmes you will need to decide on their appropriateness.

Thinking points

● As an adult, it's relatively easy to distinguish appropriate children's TV programmes (those which have an educational undercurrent at some level) from the rest which are mostly imported cartoons. These cartoons frequently have a commercial drive and they are often linked to a wide variety of merchandising. The cartoons tend to be fast moving with a lot of action. They are often clearly aimed at either boys or girls, unlike the more 'appropriate' programmes which generally strive to be gender neutral. Inevitably, children tend to like the cartoons better than the 'appropriate programmes'.

Tips, ideas and activities

● Before you decide which programme to focus on, talk to the children about their TV watching habits and favourite programmes. Ask your reluctant readers to collect information about everyone's favourite programmes and use the information to create a chart. Use information from the chart when you are deciding which programme to watch.

● TV programmes can either be watched directly from the television, on DVD/video or from TV channel websites. Many children's programmes also have an interactive, digital element. If this applies to your chosen programme explore how this feature enhances the learning process.

● Once children have watched the programme together, follow this up with a range of activities:
- Sequencing and storytelling activities.
- Drama and role play.
- Drawing and writing.
- Circle time discussions about any moral issues or choices that arose during programme.
- Transcribe part of the script and present it to children as a playscript.

● Make books or read the tie-in books with your reluctant readers. Children's prior knowledge of the characters and events should stand them in good stead to read with more confidence.

● Make links like these to TV as often as is appropriate. This will have several advantages: it shows the children that you are interested in their cultural experiences; it makes clear links between learning at home and learning in school. Above all, children's motivation to read and find out more about the adventures of their favourite characters is often higher than their motivation to find out about characters in reading books.

You Can... **Read from film**

There are so many good films for children these days and most of them are available on DVD shortly after their general cinema release. Use films as a way in to talking about characters and settings as well as to distinguish main plots and sub-plots. You can use short films, extracts from a familiar film or full-length cinema films.

Thinking points

● Does your school have a licence to watch commercial videos and DVDs that are sold for use in the home? If not, you need to get one before you use films as a way in to develop skills for reading.

● Think about when and where you are going to screen your film. This will partly depend on what you want the children to gain from the experience. If you simply want a shared 'text' to discuss together, then sitting in front of the interactive whiteboard will be enough; if you want the children to gain a cinema experience could you convert your classroom into a cinema for the afternoon? Move tables out of the way, put seats in rows, make the blackout as good as possible, use a torch like an old-fashioned usherette… .Your efforts are often reflected in the children's response to the event.

Tips, ideas and activities

● The revised *Framework for Literacy* recognises the importance of multimodal learning and you will find it relatively easy to tie-in your film experience with recommended literacy topics. The EYFS recognises the importance of using language for thinking, imagining and creativity so using film is appropriate in Reception classes too.

● Talk to your children about the films they watch. What do they make of them? Are they always able to tell you about the main events in a film?

● Depending on the age of your children, decide how long a film you wish to watch together and whether you will watch the whole film or an extract. Before you choose an extract, try to ensure that all children know the film well enough for the extract to make sense.

● You can use film in a variety of different ways, depending on your objective:
  ○ Talk about an aspect of the film: plot, characters, setting, the use of music, use of colour, use of language and humour.
  ○ Let children make 'notes' as they watch key points again. The notes can be pictures or writing but should record a response to your focus.
    ○ Ask children to bring in books of the film. Use pictures from the books – ideally stills from the film – to talk more about your focus topic.
    ○ Ask children to draw storyboards to show a sequence of events from the film. Explain to them that storyboards were invented by film-makers to show what would happen in a film.
    ○ Let children draw their storyboards in black fibre-tipped pen. If different children draw different aspects of the film, you can create a very dramatic frieze of the storyboard of a film.

You Can... **Read using computer games**

Computer games are often an ideal way to engage your reluctant, but otherwise relatively competent, reader. Many computer games rely on reading, as the character the children control has to make choices about which action to take. Although some games just depend on shooting, there are others which make heavy demands on reading for success in the game and these can be a motivating way in to reading for reluctant readers.

Thinking points

● How much are children's parents willing to help with reading? And how much will they help when the reading is on-screen, from a computer game? Although this is a fantastically successful way of encouraging many children to read, it requires intensive adult support in the early stages, as children will become quickly frustrated if they can't make sense of what is happening on-screen.

● Encourage parents to continue with computer game activities at home. This can also be a very good way of developing 'Dads 'n' Lads' bonding sessions. If your computer suite is open to the community, why not have a special Dads 'n' Lads session?

Tips, ideas and activities

● Can you get hold of a second-hand games module from one of the parents? If not, use PC games. Either way, ensure that the game is linked up so that your interactive whiteboard becomes the monitor.

● Visit a good games shop or take advice from your software supplier, parents or older pupils – you want to ensure that you find a range of games that have an element of reading but enough action to keep the children engrossed. Look on-line too, including some of the subscription websites. Most websites will allow you a month or so of free access so you can evaluate them before you commit to the fee. These are likely to be a better source of games for younger children.

● Introduce the game on the interactive whiteboard so that all children engage with the context and the opening events.

● Put children into discussion groups as they watch the interactive whiteboard so that each group can discuss choices presented once the on-screen text has been read.

● Let all the children evaluate the choices made. Teach them how to listen to others' opinions and to respond appropriately, even if they disagree. Model how to disagree politely without showing dislike or disdain for the individual.

● Use the game as the basis for drama through role play, encouraging children to explore characterisation and potential plots beyond those presented in the game.

● Use the drama to develop writing activities and allow children opportunities to read aloud from their writing so that they can share their game extension ideas with the others.

● Teach appropriate literacy objectives around the game. This is true multimodal literacy, where reading has a clear and distinct purpose.

You Can... **Read for information on-line**

The internet is now very much a part of everyday life and most children are becoming confident users. They need to be taught how to safely navigate or 'read' web pages in order to search for and find relevant information. There is information available on-line that is suitable for even the youngest of information seekers

Thinking points

● Encyclopaedias and even dictionaries are fast becoming obsolete in many children's search for information: they generally find on-line encyclopaedias more easily accessible. It is important that children know how to use the paper version of reference tools too, but for young reluctant readers, the internet is likely to be more motivating.

● How often do you ask children to seek out information independently? This doesn't include them answering your questions, but trying to find answers to their own or to each others' questions? If you are trying to create a community of learners or to develop enquiring minds in children, it is important to teach them to find information on-line – though they will need to be directed to appropriate sources.

Tips, ideas and activities

● Create a classroom library of age appropriate reference CD-ROMs and teach your children how to use them.

● Look on-line for subscription websites which are suitable for your children. Many of them will allow you free or restricted access while you evaluate the site.

● Bookmark useful reference websites that you know work in school and are allowed by your safety-screening application. Teach children how to use the bookmark to find sites you have selected.

● Use literacy or ICT time to teach children how to read a website or on-screen text. Although teachers have generally become more aware of the need to teach different skills for reading fiction and non-fiction texts types, many don't explicitly teach reading skills for websites and on-screen texts. For example:
  ○ Ensure that your children understand how to move back and forth between pages, how to close a page, how to minimise it – and they know when these actions are appropriate.
  ○ Check that children recognise hotspots (when the cursor turns into a hand) and that they know what to do with them.
  ○ Talk about all of the text on the screen including the url, the icons at the top of the screen, the labels that indicate which screen you are reading, any breadcrumb trails…
  ○ Ensure that children know what the function of each different kind of text is so that they know what they need to focus on and what they can generally ignore.
  ○ Use *Multimodal Texts* for literacy (Scholastic) to teach reading these texts.

You Can... Sequence pictures

At the earliest stages of reading comprehension, children need to understand how a text 'works'. With fiction, this generally means developing an understanding of cause and effect as well as the sequence of events within a story. With non-fiction, this generally means developing a logical understanding of progressive stages, be it the growth of a tadpole into an adult frog or the steps for making a cake. Even before children begin to read, this important understanding can be developed through sequencing activities.

Thinking points

● Have you got any kind of visual timetable on display in your classroom? Many children on the SEN register, as well as those who may be anxious or disruptive in class, can be helped by a simple visual chart showing a map of the day. These can be made on whiteboards or using little pictures fixed onto a larger card with strips or spots of Velcro®. Start with a 'Now, Next, Later' chart and stick on pictures to show, for example: *Now, we are on the carpet. Next, we will do work in our books. Later we will go to assembly.* A chart showing the whole day is the logical follow on once children have understood the Now, Next, Later idea. This is a fundamental sequencing activity which is meaningful to the children insofar as it gives them important and useful information.

Tips, ideas and activities

● At the age of four or five, many children won't consistently manage to sequence beyond three events, especially if the events they are sequencing are removed from their immediate lives. By the time they are seven years old, five or six picture cards are the maximum children are likely to sequence unless they are sequencing photographs of their own activities. Bear this in mind as you gradually extend the number of cards that the children are reordering.

● Use wordless books which are generally included in early reading schemes. The sequencing is already complete in these books, but the challenge is still to explain the sequence of events – or possibly to suggest alternative sequences of events.

● Cut up tatty copies of reading books in order to create sequencing cards. Work with the children to decide which pictures are important in creating the story and which pictures are can be left out. Once children have read the story in a reading book, let them sequence the pictures and justify their ordering.

● Buy sets of sequencing cards. Many of these show familiar sequences of events at school. Let children sequence the cards and then compare this sequence to their own experience.

● Take photographs while the children are completing activities such as cooking and craft. Print out the photographs and ask children to put them in the right order. If you allow the children to talk their way through the experience, they can generally sequence more pictures successfully.

You Can... **Encourage creative responses to stories**

In addition to using pictures for sequencing, you can employ a variety of other strategies to consider ideas and events in stories. As well as recreating the events that happened in a story, you can envisage alternative events and create new characters; you can explore what might have happened if something had been different; you can get to know the characters and settings in quite different ways. Giving children opportunities to experience alternative events in stories can be a powerful motivator in helping them to want to have these experiences for themselves as readers.

Thinking points

● How can you persuade children to want to become readers themselves? Creating, nurturing and feeding a desire to read need to be your top priorities as a teacher. As well as teaching children reading skills you need to initiate a passion for reading in your children. To do this you have to ensure that children understand why people read and realise the pleasure they can gain from reading. This may be a more difficult challenge than teaching phonics.

● In order for children to fully experience books, they need to learn that stories go 'beyond the page'. Good writers create and weave the magic of the story so that the reader wants to enter the world of the story.

Tips, ideas and activities

● Make time everyday to read good quality stories to your children. The end of the day may not be the best time for this as children may be tired. Why not make an additional time in the day for active reading where you can develop a joined response to the stories you read?

● Make a collection of toys from car boot sales and the corners of the classroom to create resources for some of your favourite stories. It won't matter to the children if the resources are out of scale with each other, or that some are old and others are new: children enjoy manipulating toys as they retell and relive stories.

● Make opportunities for your children to paint and draw in response to a story. Can they paint a setting based on information in the story? Can they draw or make different versions of a character so that they can decide which one they like best?

● Listen to a story and agree on some music that adds to the emotional engagement of the listener. Try reading the story with the music playing softly in the background. *At what point in the story does the music need to change? How is the change signalled in the text?*

● Create opportunities for drama. This is a key strand running throughout the revised *Framework for Literacy* and however much you may like or dislike drama, your children will benefit from opportunities to use their entire bodies to create a character and role play events from the story.

You Can... **Match text to pictures**

As soon as children begin to read we need to help them to understand that reading is about making meaning. Throughout Letters and Sounds, there is an emphasis on the fact that knowledge of phonics should lead to the automatic recognition of words which in turn is essential for reading comprehension: if children are working too hard to decode individual words they may have no cognitive capacity left to understand the text as a whole. Automatic word recognition is the first step towards making meaning.

Thinking points

● Talk to your children about the pictures in the books you read together. Discuss the text on each page and talk about whether each picture simply reflects the text or whether it adds more information. Do children recognise that sometimes the pictures almost tell the story better than the text does?

● Consider all the different pictures that could have been drawn to illustrate a story. Discuss questions like: *Why did the illustrator draw this event rather than a different one? Which details would you have included if you were the illustrator? Which is the most difficult word to read on this page? Does the picture always have to give clues about this word?*

Tips, ideas and activities

● Encourage children to become illustrators of books that you make together. Sometimes the child may be the author of the text, but they can also illustrate little texts that you write in order to demonstrate a particular teaching point. For example, illustrating texts such as, 'A horse with a sore hoof, walking through a door in a storm.' could be the basis for revising and reinforcing knowledge of words containing the *or* phoneme.

  ○ Make a little book out of A4 or A3 paper, or keep your text in boxes on a sheet of paper.
  ○ Write the text – don't worry about the quality of your text (the children won't) – the objective is to create a book together not necessarily to create great literature.
  ○ Let the children read the text to you in guided reading.
  ○ As some children are reading, others can begin to illustrate the story. The challenge is to make the illustrations reflect the events in the text. This involves making decisions which are not just about the individual picture, but which are about the whole book, so an understanding of the entire shape of the story is important.

● By writing your own stories, you can tailor the text to meet the reading attainment and interests of the children. What's more, if you write the stories, no one in the class will have read or illustrated these books before. This can be important for reluctant readers.

● Many reading schemes now include photocopiable resources which include pictures from a book for sequencing activities. Use these, as well as pages from tatty reading books, to create picture cards. Write accompanying text or use the original text from the reading book so that children are reading the pictures, reading the text and matching the two.

You Can... **Find the main idea**

If you talk to children about stories or films, you realise how often they have been distracted by a minor event and haven't managed to find or understand the main idea of the text. This doesn't matter too much while they are so young because it hasn't affected their enjoyment of the experience, but as children grow older and reading becomes more critical, it becomes more important that they should understand the main idea in a text.

Thinking points

● Very often, teachers find it hard to ask children questions like *What do you think that text is about?* because it they might have difficulty in articulating the answer themselves. For different texts, there are various ways of asking questions about the main idea and it is important that you are ready to model an answer if the children can't manage it themselves. If you can both ask and answer a specific question, then you can probably elicit a good answer from the children.

● Non-fiction texts are easier to use to begin with, not least because these texts generally have answers which can help to identify the main idea.

Tips, ideas and activities

● Introduce the notion of a text having a 'main idea' only after you have shared and explored the text together as it is important that the children are very familiar with a text beforehand.

● Ask different children what they think the main idea of a non-fiction text is and record their ideas verbatim.

● Explore each of the children's ideas, giving the whole class (including the children whose ideas you write down) opportunities to evaluate the ideas and express their opinions. Try to engage as many children as possible at this stage.

● Agree that the best main idea for the text is a statement which shows the idea that links the whole text together.

● Try finding the main idea in other familiar non-fiction texts. Don't worry if your main-idea sentence isn't a sentence from the text – just as long as it summarises the linking theme.

● Give children a multiple-choice activity where you prepare competing main-idea statements, each of which has some relevance to the text. Model how to evaluate the statements for the children, in order to agree on the best one.

● Give children independent opportunities to identify the main idea using multiple-choice.

● Once you have introduced the vocabulary and explored the concept of 'main idea', use it in the classroom. When you have finished talking to the children, ask them to turn to their neighbour and agree on the main idea of what you have just said; children can find the main idea from instructions, from stories and from films. This is a key concept for children to engage with.

You Can... **Explore what's *not* been said**

Inference and deduction, which are higher order reading skills, are generally assumed to be difficult and only taught to competent readers. But in order to make sense of any text, readers have to both infer and deduce – in fact, inferring is often one of the most enjoyable parts of reading – especially when you mainly read picture books and other books with a high level of illustration.

Thinking points

● The difference between inference and deduction is that when you infer, you have to read between the lines and make assumptions; when you deduce, you find clues in the text from which you draw your conclusion.

● The reason for introducing inference and deduction to children before they are competent readers is to equip them with tools they will need later. If children are used to actively reading a text, with a full understanding of the nuances and suppositions that they are being asked to make, then this becomes a reading habit. The fact that the 'texts' they are being asked to read at this stage are not written texts, but texts which they hear or see does not minimise their importance.

Tips, ideas and activities

● Introduce the idea that whenever you share a book together, you gather information from a number of sources: the first is the text itself; then there are probably pictures; and finally you use information from your own experience and understanding to complete the meaning that you make.

● Agree different words to talk about the different level of meaning, for example: *it's there in the writing; it's there in the pictures; work it out; what do you think?*

● As you read texts aloud, ask questions at the different levels of meaning and ask the children both to respond to the questions and to let you know which level of meaning each question addresses.

● In addition to identifying these levels of meaning in written text, use them to talk about pictures too. Find picture books you haven't yet read and talk about some of the pictures using different levels of meaning: *it's there in the writing; it's there in the pictures; work it out; what do you think?*

● Use ideas from your discussions of two or three pictures from a book to see if you can predict something about the story. Read the story and see how well your predictions worked.

● Once children are beginning to read more fluently, ask them oral questions at each of the different levels so they become used to actively thinking about what they are reading and how they are making meaning. Teach them strategies so that they understand that when they are answering an *It's there in the text* question, they should be able to identify words and phrases from the text in their answer. When they are answering a *What do you think* question, however, they may not be able to point directly to one sentence which will give them the answer.

You Can... **Read poetry together**

Given how much children tend to enjoy poetry, it's surprising how little of it is read in school. For reluctant readers, poems are very good texts partly because they are often short, but also because the rhythm and rhyme help to make the text memorable. If you share poems at various times during the day with your class, that also gives poetry a high status which means that children will be more eager to read it.

Thinking points
● Which kinds of poetry books are in your class library? Do the children have easy access to high quality and well illustrated anthologies of appropriate poems and rhymes?

● Many children today arrive in school without knowing nursery and counting rhymes, so it becomes even more important to make them available. In addition to playing counting and finger rhymes, it's also useful to show children these rhymes in picture books and anthologies so that they can find them and take pleasure in knowing that they can 'read' their poem in a book. Publication gives these rhymes status in the children's eyes.

Tips, ideas and activities
● Put books of poems and rhymes out on tables for children to look at and to talk about. Make this a legitimate activity so that the children are not snatching time to read poems, but time is allocated for reading at length.

● Talk about how poems are different from prose. Can children recognise a poem when they see it printed? How do they know it's a poem?

● Read a wide variety of poems to your class. Children very often enjoy nonsense poems and these are likely to be among the first poems that your reluctant readers will read for themselves, but also give them experience of hearing longer and more descriptive poems.

● There are many poems which we might read to young children in which the language or some of the words are archaic. Don't be put off. As long as the children can understand the main idea of the poem, it won't matter too much if some of the language is challenging. Sometimes, the experience of hearing the richness of the language can inspire children even if they don't know what the individual words mean.

● Let children doodle as you read poems to them. Later, ask them to turn some of the doodles into pictures or paintings which express the feelings in the poem. As they do this, offer children opportunities to paint on wet paper or to draw and paint using different media. In this way they can explore ways of reflecting ideas both in words and through creative media.

● If you can, invite a performance poet into school. This will undoubtedly encourage even the most reluctant of readers to have a go at reading some of the poems – particularly the funny ones.

BEWARE THE JABBERWOCK MY SON!

You Can... **Play with rhyme**

Playing with rhyme is a key part of Phase 1 of Letters and Sounds, but it is a game that can continue throughout Key Stage 1. Not only is rhyme – and an awareness of the sounds in language – a key skill for successful reading, but it is one of the most versatile and enjoyable aspects of teaching reading.

Thinking points

● Research in the mid-1980s suggested that awareness of rhyme is a key indicator as to likely future success with reading. The argument was that pre-school children first hear running speech which they learn to separate into the biggish chunks of sound which are individual words. Later, children hear the next biggest chunk of sound which is rhyme and only after that do they begin to hear the small chunks of sound which are the individual phonemes.

● As well as training the ear to hear the sounds, rhyming activities can also train the eye to see spelling patterns. Reading and spelling using analogy is not foolproof, but it is a useful strategy.

Tips, ideas and activities

● Nonsense poems are a great place to start when beginning to read using rhyme and analogy since the lines are predictable and, for some reason, memorable. Poems like Spike Milligan's 'On the Ning Nang Nong' lend themselves very readily to reading games. These could include:
  ● Reading the poem.
  ● Taking out every second line, writing them on separate pieces of paper and asking children to use the rhyming words as a clue to putting all the lines back again.
  ● Mixing sets of lines up and asking the children to put them back into rhyming couplets.
  ● Covering up some of the lines and asking children to suggest new lines.
  ● Comparing words like *ning, nang* and *nong* and talking about what makes them look the same and what is different and then inventing rhyming words for each or them.

● Nursery rhymes also have great potential for reading and rhyming. For example you could:
  ● Change the rhyming word at the end of a line and explore how the rhyme needs to change.
  ● Teach one word in a rhyming pair and ask children to read another.
  ● Make sets of words which rhyme from a poem.
  ● Give children a percussion instrument: ask them to play it when they hear a word that rhymes with another word they have just heard.

● As well as starting with existing poems and rhymes, you could make sets of rhyming words as a starting point and create your own rhymes around them.

● As well as using commercial games of rhyming snap, lotto and pairs, begin to collect sets of objects and pictures which you can sort into sets of words that rhyme.

● Many children need a lot of experience with rhyme and find it a tricky concept to understand. It is important to keep rehearsing rhymes and rhyming activities in order to support children while they become more comfortable with rhyme.

You Can... **Recognise rhythm and beat**

Rhythm is a fundamental part of most human societies and it is one of the most distinguishing characteristics of a language. In English, for example, we tend to put the stress on the first syllable of a word, unless the word has a prefix at the beginning. Playing with rhythm is great fun for young children but the links with reading are well researched. Helping children to learn more about rhythm through poetry and rhyme is a natural and enjoyable way of practising this important skill.

Thinking points

● The 'rhythm' in a song or poem reflects the syllables in each word and the 'beat' is the steady pulse that continues throughout an entire line or verse. For example, the line *Humpty Dumpty sat on a wall.* has a rhythm of eight unevenly stressed and spaced syllables, whereas there are a steady four beats. There are generally between two and four beats in a line of simple poetry.

● The quickest way to find out which of your children can identify the beat is to ask them to clap in time to a song: we always clap the beat.

● Hearing the rhythm of language is critical when children begin to read words with more than one syllable as altering the stress pattern and rhythm of the word can make it sound very different.

Tips, ideas and activities

● Link teaching about beat and rhythm as a reading skill with music lessons. Children will indubitably feel more motivated to explore these concepts when they have access to percussion instruments.

● Try clapping the opening lines of a familiar song or nursery rhyme. Can children work out which one it is? If necessary, help their thinking by giving them a choice of two rhymes. To begin with, you could give choices of rhymes with two very different rhythms to make guessing easier (for example, 'Humpty Dumpty' and 'Hey Diddle Diddle').

● Can your children work together but do something different? Can one half of them keep a steady beat going while the other half claps to the rhythm of the poem or song?

● Once children are familiar with a poem, ask them to read it aloud while you keep a steady beat going. This activity may help children whose reading is too slow – but beware of hurrying them too much because that will put them under too much pressure.

● Encourage children to work together to perform a poem or nursery rhyme. All of the children should read different parts of the rhyme while the others maintain a beat using body percussion.

● Use songs and poems as the basis for exploring syllables in longer words. For example, in the song 'The Animals went in Two by Two', there's a phrase which goes *...the elephant and the kangaroo.* Explore how many other animal names you could sing in the same space within that line for example: ants *wolves, frogs and some monkeys too.*

● Introduce poems with longer words. Children are very often frightened of reading words with more than one syllable because they look harder: if they have met long words in familiar poems they are less likely to be scared of them.

You Can... **Read line by line**

Unlike any other medium, poetry is very compelling because of the close relationship that one line has with the next. This gives us a unique opportunity to work with words where the reader feels compelled to know what's going to come next because without a satisfying completion, there's a definite unfinished feeling. It's almost as if entire poems are composed of cliff-hanger endings! We can exploit this trait to motivate reluctant readers.

Thinking points
● Children need to experience a wide variety of poems being read aloud to them in order that they can understand that poems have different constructions and that not all poems rhyme or have a clear rhythm and beat. It's interesting to consider why some poets – like Michael Rosen – generally choose to write poems rather than paragraphs of prose, and what would change if they did.

● Use poems and rhymes to enliven almost any topic that you are looking at in school. The children will enjoy the poems and rhymes and even your reluctant readers may begin to try to read them if they are on display and sufficiently familiar.

Tips, ideas and activities
● Teach children a poem which has a repetitive refrain. Read the poem and let the children read the refrain. This is a very inclusive activity which allows all of the children in the class to feel that they are participating and contributing.

● Let children choose poems they enjoy. Photocopy the poem, or put it on the interactive whiteboard, for a group of children to read aloud to the class, one line at a time. Talk about whether or not this is effective.

● Copy out a poem, writing one line at a time on each of several stepping stones. Create a pathway of the stepping stones across the floor. (Make sure that the stepping stones are not slippery to stand on.) Let children move along the pathway, reading the poem one line at a time. This works well with both rhyming poetry, where the children need to find the rhymes, and with non-rhyming poetry where children need to finish the thought or idea.

● Give each child one line from a poem to read and illustrate. Create poetry books showing each line with its illustration. Keep the poetry books in your school or class library so that the children can read and reread their favourite poems and look at the illustrations.

● Use one line from a poem as the basis for developing a new poem. Try to begin with a descriptive line and see where the children's imagination takes them. Post the poem(s) you create onto a website such as www.childrenspoetrybookshelf.co.uk and read poems written by other children and classes.

● Introduce some of the more accessible 'classic poems' and teach lines and verses from them to the children so that they can recite at least one line. Make sure they are to some extent familiar with these poems.

HAD A GREAT FALL

HUMPTY DUMPTY

SAT ON A WALL

HUMPTY DUMPTY

You Can... **Hold your own poetry award**

There are a significant number of book awards these days which tend to be for fiction books, whether they are aimed at adults or children. Why don't you create a class or school poetry award? Consider the main benefit: all the children will read a number of poems on the shortlist in order to vote for their favourite. Additional benefits include the status of poetry being raised in your class or school and that children will begin to talk about poems. You could even link your poetry award with raising money for the school in the form of sponsorship for poetry-related events and activities.

Thinking points

● Before introducing the idea to the children, you will also need to consider logistical issues like how all the children are going to manage to read the poems? You will need to have access to a substantial number of copies of the poems you intend to shortlist. Even if every class in the school nominates two poems to a shortlist, you will still need to make the poems available to everybody else. In order that you aren't infringing any copyright laws, you may wish to contact either the poet or the publisher and ask their permission to use their poem in your award. If the poem is already available on-line from, for example, www.gigglepoetry.com or www. poemhunter.com then direct children to the relevant web pages; check terms and conditions of the websites before displaying or printing material.

Tips, ideas and activities

● Inevitably, a whole-school poetry award can't happen without the goodwill of the staff who need to be prepared to make it an exciting event and to help the children to want to participate. Your first task is therefore to encourage everyone to get involved and publicise the event.

● Once you have all the details sorted out, introduce the idea to the children.

● Clarify how many poems each class – or group of children if it's just your class – can nominate. Try to have a shortlist of no more than five to ten poems.

● Agree how the children in your class or each group are going to nominate their poems. Are they going to select by reading the poems aloud in their groups, by reading the poems to each other or by listening to you read the poems aloud?

● Check that all of the children understand the idea of voting. They won't all have their choice of poem selected and some of them might find this difficult.

● Once all of the poems for the shortlist have been selected, revisit the selection process within your class so that all of the children have the opportunity to hear the poems on the shortlist.

● Ensure that the award announcement is made into an exciting event. Can you invite a local celebrity to announce the winner?

● If the winner is a living poet, why not invite them to come to school to collect their award?

You Can... **Create a story world**

Today's children live in a very visual world: at home, they watch cartoons, they play computer games, they are privileged to have access to a wide variety of richly illustrated picture books and they can even re-enact stories by buying and playing with character figures. In school, teachers have to compete with and match this level of visual stimulation for their reluctant readers otherwise reading may be disregarded as 'boring'.

Thinking points

● Very few children will now say that they prefer TV to radio 'because the pictures are better'. The closest many children ever get to listening to stories on the radio, is their experience of listening to stories on audio cassette as they go to sleep. Do you ever tell stories, or read stories that are not illustrated? Are your children dependent on illustrations to enter a story world?

● Although it may seem like a lot of work to recreate and develop story worlds in school, it may be a way into reading for some of your reluctant readers. Some of these children don't find it easy to use the language or imaginative powers necessary to enter into an invented world and for them, this can be a barrier to reading.

Tips, ideas and activities

● Before you recreate the world of a story within your classroom, you need to consider which story you intend to work on: ideally, you will choose a story that has more than one book version and a setting which lends itself to extended ideas and stories. This can develop into a rich source of opportunities for developing speaking and listening.

● Are you going to make your story world classroom-sized, table-sized, display-sized, or picture-sized? The answer to this question will partly depend on the books(s) you choose, on the age of your children and on resources available to you.

● Classroom story worlds are effectively an extension of a role-play area across a wider area of the classroom. Within this context you can make ice caves, dinosaur swamps, post offices, different places within an island, castles, temples and so on. Once the area is decorated and furnished with appropriate props and clothes, your can all re-enact stories and develop new ideas around characters.

● Small-world toys can also be used to create story worlds. Children are generally unconcerned with scale and manufacturer, so a mixture of characters made up from different sets of toys, perhaps clothed in some fabric scraps can provide a rich environment for groups of children to work together to retell stories.

● Individual children's pictures, at whatever scale, can also provide extended story worlds: reread the story so that children can remember the features that the author has already thought of and then ask children to add their own ideas. Characters can be drawn or cut out to make collages.

● Whichever level of story world you decide to use, allow children to talk as they work together: their talk is how they really begin to engage in these new worlds.

You Can... **Write exciting snippets**

The aim of the back cover blurb is to draw the reader in so that they want to read the book. When asked about their impressions of a book, children will often suggest something about the book which is entirely different from that chosen for the blurb. Let children write and share their own blurbs to recommend books to others to read.

Thinking points

● Most children find writing book reviews to be an unfulfilling activity. It often has no clear audience and the comments they are invited to suggest are constrained by the writing frame. Teachers who are reading the book reviews rarely acquire insights into the children's enjoyment of the book. Focusing the activity to writing a blurb for a favourite book can be much more liberating for the reviewer and can create a sense of excitement in prospective readers.

● If we want reluctant readers to engage in reading, recommendations for favourite books that come from peers are much more likely to be taken up than any reading list provided by the school. Recommendations which are provided in the form of blurbs or snippets are particularly powerful.

Tips, ideas and activities

● Read blurbs together. Talk about 'what makes a good blurb': is it more likely to be a question, a comment, an extract, a recommendation or a picture? Look at all the different kinds of blurb on various books and discuss which makes you want to read the book.

● Teach the children to read, to think of, and to write questions. Discuss the difference between types of questions, for example, *What did the caterpillar eat? Did the caterpillar like chocolate cake? What does a caterpillar do if it has stomach-ache? Which of these questions makes you want to read the book more?* Discuss why.

● Look at examples of persuasive language in blurbs, for example: 'Read this book if you want to laugh all night long!' Compare them to statements like: 'You can find out about caterpillars if you read this book.' Talk about which is more effective and why. Point out features of persuasive texts (use of command verbs at the beginning and their strong positive voice).

● Talk about the kinds of extracts you might want to use to entice someone to read a book. Is it more likely to be 'Time was running out for Joe and Beth. Their only hope was to climb the cliffs that reached high above the boiling sea' or 'One sunny morning, Joe and Beth went to the seaside'?

● Once you have explored different kinds of blurbs, help children to develop their own ideas through:
  - Modelling – write a few different blurbs for a shared read and ask children to select the most successful and to explain why.
  - Applying – after a shared reading session, work in shared and guided writing sessions to create joint blurbs.
  - Practising – let the children write their own blurbs for books they have enjoyed.
  - Evaluating – the children can vote for the blurb that they find most interesting. Only talk together about those deemed successful.

You Can... **Select books to read aloud**

Reading aloud to your class is probably the most positive thing you can do to encourage them to read. Your children are probably still at the stage where they want to 'please teacher', and part of that involves liking what you like – so if you enjoy reading, and you share your enthusiasm with them, you are already sending them strong and positive messages about the value, importance and enjoyment of reading.

Thinking points

● You were probably read to as a child both at home and at school. This shared reading experience was formative for many young children because not only did it take place in a safe and happy environment, but it invited children to participate with others in co-creating a world and shared experience which could stretch beyond the duration of the reading itself.

● For many children nowadays, the DVD, story tape or CD-ROM has replaced the bedtime story book, so this makes your job of enabling children to experience the social aspect of reading aloud together so much more important.

● Young children are often insufficiently literate to experience the magic of a story world for themselves. By reading aloud, you give them access to that world – and that's vital if teachers are to help create a generation of children who enjoy reading.

Tips, ideas and activities

● Once every term or so, visit a good bookshop or children's library with a friend or colleague. Spend time exploring new children's books together in a relaxed manner: have a drink, share the books you enjoy, find out about new illustrators and authors, while also checking on your favourites. More and more children's books are being published each year and it is useful for you to keep up with the best of them. Comparing books, handling them and taking time to explore text and illustrations are experiences which will help you to choose books which you know you can use to inspire your class.

● If you can't get to a good bookshop yourself, explore recommendations made by independent specialist booksellers. Try going to www.literacytrust.org.uk for a list (not exhaustive) of specialist booksellers. Even if there isn't one near you, you will at least be able to read reviews and perhaps then you can request a book from a non-specialist bookshop or your local library.

● Visit 'book fairs' at www.scholastic.co.uk to organise a Scholastic Book Fair in school. Knowing that the books are on sale then and there to take home is a tremendous incentive for young children.

● When reading aloud to the children, use all your latent dramatic skills – all teachers are performers. Make it 'live' for them. Use anything you can think of to grip the children: vary the pace and pitch of your voice; speak, stand and move in character; create tension and drama; use props if they're helpful; address individual children directly as you read. You are probably the key to unlocking the habit of reading in many of your children.

● Consider reading more often than just at the end of the day when the children tend to be tired and ready to go home. It's rarely the best time to share with them the most important secret of all – the need to read.

You Can... **Find out about authors and illustrators**

In spite of all the work we do in school, children often fail to understand that authors and illustrators are ordinary people too. Knowing about these people can inspire some children to want to be like them – it can be their motivation to practise reading and writing.

Thinking points

● Who were your favourite authors or illustrators when you were growing up? Did you – or do you still – feel a frisson when you find a book by a favourite author that you haven't yet read? Did you – or do you still – have books whose pages are falling out because you have read that same book over and over again? Can you think back as to what it was/is about that author or illustrator that so gripped your imagination?

● For many children, it won't necessarily be the 'good books' or the best children's literature that turns on their reading button – it may well be TV tie-in comics, or wordless books, or a particular style or design of non-fiction book. It is important, particularly for the reluctant readers, that we celebrate any interaction with print and offer opportunities to pursue and extend it.

Tips, ideas and activities

● Use your school library service: ask them to put together a book box containing books which are linked by a particular author or illustrator which you think will interest your children.

● Try to find posters profiling specific authors or illustrators. Again, ask your library service but you may also find posters from bookshops or on-line: try the National Literacy Trust at www.literacytrust.org.uk or contact the publishers. Many publishers will happily provide posters for your classroom at no cost.

● Collect together as many of the relevant books by a particular author as you can and make an interactive display. Encourage children to spend time exploring it. Allow planned time in literacy or quiet reading where you have an expectation that children will explore the books and information on the display. The more attractive you make this display the more likely children are to use it.

● Write an author or illustrator quiz and give a prize. Depending on the age of your children, this could be as simple as asking children to carry out a treasure hunt or write a list of books by a particular author or it could be more complex with an expectation that children will read and respond to an author/illustrator interview.

● Talk about expectations of the author or illustrator. Authors in particular tend to write books from a particular angle: is the named author likely to write books about family life, books about animals, books about fighting, adventure stories, funny stories or non-fiction books? Use these conversations to help children to develop an understanding of different genre as well as the difference between fiction and non-fiction books.

You Can... Invite an author or illustrator into school

Many children's authors and illustrators are willing to supplement their income and meet their readers by doing school visits. This can be an exciting event for the children, especially if you make it so. Some authors cite visits to schools where the teachers appeared uninterested and the children seemed bemused. However, they can also cite more visits where the teachers had prepared the children well for the visit and made the visitor feel both welcome and special.

Thinking points

● If you want to invite a 'big name' visitor, especially if they don't live near you, you may want to join forces with a neighbouring school because the visit won't be cheap and you will need to pay accommodation and travel costs too. If, however, you want a published author or illustrator to come and talk about the process of writing and publishing a book, you are likely to be able to find someone who lives within a reasonable day's travel to your school. Remember that they generally work for fees or royalties on a freelance basis and they have to earn a living!

Tips, ideas and activities

● Before you set out to invite a guest into school, you need to think carefully about what you want from them. Are they just for entertainment in order for children to appreciate that real people write books and draw pictures, or are you hoping that the children will learn something specific from the visit? Do you want a talk, a book reading session, a writing workshop? Each of these different visits will have different implications for your children and your visitor.

● Once you have decided on the purpose, you need to contact the author. As a first stop you might want to try www.contactanauthor.co.uk which will help you to locate authors near where you live. The National Literacy Trust also produces a free booklet on inviting writers into schools, Download it for free at www.literacytrust.org.uk.

● There are also agencies who will undertake to contact the author and set up the day for you, freeing you from all of the administrative details for example www.classactagency.co.uk or www.jubileebooks.co.uk are two agencies. Look for others on the internet since they each represent authors who have signed up with them.

● Many publishers will also put you in touch with their authors or, if you have a particular author in mind, you can often contact them through their own web page.

● It is important to prepare your children for the author visit: read their books, plan questions to ask, look the author up on the internet so that you all know something about them.

● You may want to offer a bookshop for the day, selling the author's books. If your local bookshop won't let you have a pile of books on sale or return, contact the author's publisher and see if they can help or contact a specialist school's bookshop (find one near you at www.literacytrust.org.uk).

You Can... **Read environmental print**

We live in a print-rich world. Children are surrounded not only by books in school, but by print from notices, newspapers, magazines, advertisements, food labels, shop sign boards and so on. Although very young children can't decode this print, many of them are aware that it carries meaning and they can recognise some places and products by the look and the logo. You can exploit these very early 'making meaning' experiences of print as early steps in teaching reading.

Thinking points

● The extent to which you want to bring environmental print into your classroom will depend partly on the age of the children you teach and on the style and set up of your classroom. However, the advantage of using environmental print as a teaching aid is that much environmental print is something which children feel a need to read because it is important to them to know what the message is.

● Before you start to bring environmental print into your curriculum, you will want to consider how it will link to other curriculum projects. This may determine the breadth of the print types you share with the children in school. You will also want to decide on which of the many purposes of environmental print you wish to focus on

Tips, ideas and activities

● Role-play areas are an easy and interactive way of bringing environmental print into the classroom. Whether you set up a role-play area as a post office, a doctors' or a vets' surgery, a garden centre, an elves' workshop, a supermarket, a garage… there are opportunities for environmental print in terms of posters, forms to write on, lists, telephone numbers and so on. In addition to supplying the print products for the children to explore and use as they will, you can also set up guided opportunities to discuss the print, its purpose and its message.

● Go on an environmental print walk around school, talking to children about what the print says and what it means. Let children copy some of the print that they think is important.

● Talk about different purposes for environmental print: How many can the children find in school? For example: there are notices with information ('We do PE on Thursdays'), instructions ('Now Wash Your Hands'), labels ('Class 3'), letters, safety information ('fire exit'). Help the children to categorise all the different kinds of information.

● Use catalogues in class. Ask children to find toys that they know about in the catalogues. Talk about the information they used to find the toys. Discuss what skills they think they are using: are they are making meaning from the print that they are reading?

● Use information from your talk about the catalogues to develop the skills that the children are already using. For example, if they are able to remember and match two similar objects, you can set up activities to extend this into matching letters or words; if they are able to match letters, you may be able to begin to develop some phonics skills. As far as possible, keep these activities linked to the catalogues, or whatever print you first used to capture the children's interest.

You Can... **Make an information tool kit**

If you want to encourage reluctant readers to use their reading skills, you need to start by making this as easy as possible. If you can give these children their own 'tool kits' in little boxes or bags, this may give literacy activities sufficient novelty and prestige to make the children want to use the tools in their kit. It would be impractical to provide these kits for every child in the class – and it would detract from their special status if you did – but for a few children and for a short time they may be stimulating.

Thinking points

● To be truly effective, an information tool kit needs to match the needs of its owner – and you. The intention is that the tool kit should be a short-term intervention to help to focus the child's mind and attention on developing skills for learning, particularly reading and writing. If the child starts to misuse the tool kit, it will stop being useful; if you don't give the child time and opportunities to use the tool kit, it will also lose its value very quickly.

● A quick visit to a DIY store will probably yield some small DIY tool boxes or open carry cases. As long as the case is large enough to hold the tools you need, but not too bulky, this kind of container is ideal – especially for boys.

Tips, ideas and activities

● The tool kit needs to contain equipment which will actually be useful to the children during the course of the day.

● All tool kits should include some basic stationery items including a pencil and a pencil sharpener. Whether or not you include an eraser will depend on your school policy and on the individual child. You may also want to include some colouring pencils. A small clean whiteboard, together with dry-wipe marker pen and wiper are also useful for most children.

● Sticky notes can also be helpful. Children can use them for noting down thoughts and for communicating with you and the other children. If you receive a sticky note, try to reply to it as this will provide an additional reason for reading.

● Include an appropriate picture dictionary so that children can browse and find words. Plastic magnifying glasses are also useful for finding information and children will usually enjoy using them.

● A laminated A4 mat should also be included. Depending on the stage of the child, it may have: letters of the alphabet with pictures; high-frequency words; words for matching; spelling and reading rules; reminders of the current literacy or Individual Educational Plan (IEP) targets.

● The tool kit may well include a little interactive activity: a high-frequency words memory game: three letter dice to throw and make CVC words; magnetic letters to manipulate to spell words. It is also possible to include numeracy activities.

● Provide opportunities to use the tool kit as often as possible during the day in order to make children feel important and to give opportunities for using and developing reading skills.

You Can... **Use computers**

Computers are now commonplace in classrooms and in many homes and most children are becoming confident users of new technologies. However, we do need to teach children the full range of what a computer can do. Part of this is teaching children to use the computer to read and retrieve information.

Thinking points

● Dictionaries are now less used by children: they generally find the electronic spell-checker more easily accessible. Although it is necessary to remind children of the importance of using book based reference materials, for young reluctant readers the computer may be more engaging.

● Do you often ask children to seek out information alone? If you want to encourage young learners to be enquiring, it is important to teach children to find and read information from a computer.

Tips, ideas and activities

● Teach even very young children how to read a computer screen. Reading from the screen involves very different skills to reading from books. Children need to know, for instance:

○ Which parts of the screen are about navigation and which parts have information or games.

○ How to exit from a screen or go back to a previous screen.

○ How to make a choice from a menu and what a screen menu looks like.

○ How the cursor changes to indicate that clicking here might change what you see.

○ Where you enter information and how you click to indicate that you are entering this information.

● Have a collection of appropriate CD-ROMs available for children to use. Make sure that children know how to load them and to treat all CD-ROMs appropriately. If you have a 'Favourites' folder available for children to use on your class computer, make sure that all of the links are live and appropriate and that children know how to access and use the folder.

● Provide prompt cards with icons beside them to allow children to read instructions to gain access to the programs.

● Encourage children to ask questions about what you discuss in the classroom and generate an expectation that having asked a question, they should try to find out the answer using a computer. Give them as little help as is appropriate for each child.

● Give children the tools they need to help them to find and to record information: writing frames into which they can write or copy key words for their search; highlighter pens so that they can highlight anything they print; written suggestions for particular places they might search for the information.

You Can... Teach children how to follow instructions

Reading to follow instructions can be one of the easiest and most motivating ways of getting children excited about reading. Instructions to follow classroom routines are especially interesting, because the routines themselves are so familiar that it takes little reading skill to work out what is probably written on the paper.

Thinking points

● Following instructions can be great fun because you engage with the text to reach the required outcomes. Instructions tend to be associated with recipes and 'how to' books, but they are used so much more widely than that. Many instructions have the conventional step-by-step structure, but if you think of the language you use to engage with your class for much of the day, you organise them through the medium of instructions.

● Instructions don't just have to take the place of sequences of actions: classroom rules are also instructional texts – they tell us what to do. Even road signs like 'STOP' and 'GIVE WAY' are instructions.

Tips, ideas and activities

● Begin by establishing a 'reading not talking' day. This could be in the context of a sponsored quiet, of a sore throat, or just of an interesting idea. Explain to the children that you plan to communicate as much as possible using signs rather than the spoken word.

● For the youngest children, give instructions using icons or photographs: when you want them to be quiet, hold up a sign showing a finger on lips; if you want them to line up, hold up a photo of them lining up; if you want them to prepare for a lesson, show them a sign of equipment for the lesson.

● Once children are beginning to look at signs, rather than listening for your voice, make the signs a mixture of words and symbols. You can either hold up the words one at a time, or in a sentence.

● Begin to use these oral and written instructions for a wide variety of daily routines. Even doing the register can involve a number of signs: 'sit still'; 'be quiet'; 'listen for your name'; 'school dinner' or 'packed lunch' and so on.

● After a while the novelty will wear off, but it's worth revisiting these reading not talking days periodically through the term.

● Give children more predictable written instructions to tell them what they are required to do. If they are working from school books or worksheets, take the time to read the rubric together – these are generally deemed to be for adults and are often ignored, but publishers try to make them accessible to children. If children have done this type of activity before, they may well successfully read what they have to do themselves.

● Find puzzle-book activities for the children. They very often enjoy solving puzzles such as, finding the odd one out, spotting three differences between the pictures, but again, take time to read the rubrics together so that children are continually practising reading for a purpose.

You Can... **Visit a library**

As library membership dwindles, libraries are closing down. Help to reverse this trend by making sure that all of your children are members of the library and that they know where the nearest library is. Libraries are a vital resource in a community and schools need to play their part in promoting their use.

Thinking points

- Before you take your class to the library, visit it yourself. This isn't just for the purpose of doing a risk assessment, but it also prepares you for the kinds of resources and activities available. Can one of the librarians – or a specialist children's librarian from the county service – arrange to spend time with your class? Do they have a range of ideas and activities available for the children or will it be your responsibility to think of things to do while at the library?

- Before your visit, ask for a pile of membership forms. If you take them back to school and have them signed by the children's parents, then return them to the library before your visit, the children can often be presented with their very own library cards when you go to the library together.

Tips, ideas and activities

- Before you visit your local library, take the children into your school library if you are lucky enough to have one. Talk about the kinds of books available in the library. Do you have both fiction and non-fiction? If so, talk about how they are shelved: it is important that children know that if they take a book off a shelf in a library, they can't just put it back on the nearest shelf. Discuss with them why they think libraries are arranged in this way.

- Establish appropriate behaviours in the library: although few public libraries insist on silence nowadays, they probably have expectations that voices will be muted to allow other library users to concentrate and they almost certainly discourage rushing around or eating and drinking near the books.

- Organise your classroom bookshelves into a library: ask children to help you to separate books into fiction and non-fiction (and while you are doing this you can discuss the criteria you use to decide which is which). Make sets of the non-fiction books so that you can shelve them together and ask some children to begin to sort fiction books into alphabetical order by the author's family name.

- During this book sorting activity, try to allow opportunities for the children to browse through the books. In many classrooms, there are too many books so children only ever look at a small number. (In some schools, classroom book stocks are limited to 50–60 books which are changed every half-term so that all of the books are available at some point.)

- Actively encourage the children and their parents to make use of your community library once you have all visited it. Advertise storytelling sessions in the holidays and weekend activities; take time to look at books borrowed from the library which support curriculum; encourage parents to borrow books to share with their children.

You Can... **Find out about reading habits**

How much do you know about your children's reading habits and preferences? Although teachers are usually aware of children's reading experiences in school, it's often much harder to know about their attitudes and beliefs about reading.

Thinking points

● In a busy classroom, it's hard enough to keep track of whose phonic knowledge is developing, who can read high-frequency words and which stage of the reading scheme each child or group is on. If your school runs a successful home reading record, you may also know how often each child reads at home to a parent. But when do you get the opportunity to sit down and to hear each child's voice? What do they think of reading? Which kinds of books do they like reading? Do they enjoy listening to stories? What do they find easy or challenging about reading? What do they like doing if they get stuck on a word? Do they have any books at home to read? Finding answers to questions like these is useful for all children, but vital when you are trying to unlock your reluctant readers.

Tips, ideas and activities

● Having time to talk to children about reading is an important part of your role as class teacher, but, finding that time can be challenging. Talking to individual children is an acceptable part of Preparation, Planning and Assessment time (PPA time in England) as a reading interview is for the purposes of assessment for learning.

● Before you begin a reading interview with a child, it's worth thinking about what precisely you are trying to find out: is this a general discussion about reading experiences? Are you trying to establish what challenges the child perceives him/herself as facing? Do you want to know about reading experiences and opportunities at home? Even though children generally trust you as their teacher, their concentration is likely to wander so it's important that you have an outcome in mind before you begin.

● Depending on the desired outcome, are you going to need books with you for your discussion? If so, will you want the child's reading book; other reading books at a similar level; fiction and non-fiction books from the class library; new and special books, perhaps from your own bookshelf at home? The books that you have available may, to some extent, influence the outcome of your reading interview, so choose them carefully.

● Where will you hold the reading interview? This is very important. It needs to be a positive and relaxed experience for both you and the child, so the room that you choose should reflect this.

● Try to keep the interview friendly and informal, so that the child feels able to share their ideas and experiences. Once you have heard the child's voice about him/herself as a reader, you should be able to make better plans for moving forwards.

You Can... Set up treasure hunts

Treasure hunts are fun. They are often best done outside in the warmer weather and they are very motivating and exciting. Organising a treasure hunt can seem like a lot of work, but if you plan your clues carefully enough – and laminate them – the same set of clues can be recycled in a different order, so a little effort now can have children reading for weeks to come.

Thinking points

● Before you plan a treasure hunt there are some obvious issues to consider around the children's safety and supervision and these factors are likely to determine the extent of the treasure hunt you can create. Will, for example, your whole class be outside all at the same time, or will you be sending them out in small groups with a trusted adult or older children?

● To some extent, the opportunities afforded by your outside space will also limit your activities. City centre schools with tarmac playgrounds will be the base for a different kind of treasure hunt than from suburban and country schools with extensive playing fields or adventure playgrounds. However, none of these constraints affect your ability to organise a treasure hunt for your children – they just impact on the space and places you can use.

Tips, ideas and activities

● Treasure hunts can take place in as small a space as a sand tray. Sandpit treasure hunts can serve a number of purposes:
  ○ To match objects with their initial letters.
  ○ To find all the letters needed to spell a word.
  ○ To match an object (in the sand) with its word (not in the sand).
  ○ To find an object and match it with a clue (for example, a plastic cat could be found to match the clue, 'I have four legs').

● Classroom or playground treasure hunts can involve more reading:
  ○ Take a photograph of a soft toy sitting in an easily identified place. Put a letter or a word in that place for children to find, record and leave.
  ○ Teach vocabulary for prepositions (*in, on, under, behind, in front, beside* and so on). Give children photographs of objects together with the preposition, or even the sentence 'Look under the…' and ask them to look there for the treasure. Again, the treasure should be something children can see, record and then leave for others to find.
  ○ Match clues to photographs (for example, 'Inside a brown pot with a hole in the bottom. Could be inside a flower pot.') and then ask children to find the object and the treasure.
  ○ Write clues to places and hide the treasure there.

● In each of these treasure hunts, children should expect to find part of the treasure at each place. They will then need to use all of the separate 'treasures' to solve some kind of a puzzle.

You Can... **Use your role-play corner**

Role-play corners can easily be transformed into places where children need to read. There are so many reasons to create 'authentic' opportunities, where children can have the kinds of reading experiences that they witness in the outside world. Consider the difference it would make to children's learning if you could extend your role-play area across your curriculum, and give all of your children regular opportunities to engage in play in this space.

Thinking points

● Role-play corners used to be common in classrooms throughout Key Stage 1, but they are becoming increasingly rare by Year 2. But many Year 2 children, particularly those who are developing more slowly than their peers, still both enjoy and benefit from opportunities to role play. These feed into children's social and emotional learning, as well as their opportunities for truly multi-sensory, self-driven learning.

● If you currently teach without a role-play corner, how might reinstating one impact on your classroom? Is there space? Can you conceive of teaching in a way that would allow children opportunities to engage in play within the area? How would the props you would need differ from those used for younger classes?

Tips, ideas and activities

● The role-play area in a classroom doesn't have to focus around 'domestic' play and may benefit, particularly for children aged over six, from having a degree of structure in the form of a task or focus to the play.

● Select the focus for your area from the wider curriculum: if you are studying 'toys', then make it into a toymaker's workshop; if you are learning about Florence Nightingale, have a hospital; if it's the Battle of Hastings then make an armourer's workshop. The focus could also come from a maths topic: when looking at time, have a clock shop and if it's money, have either a supermarket, a café, a toy shop or a catalogue shop. A simple idea in geography could also be developed through a travel agent's or a post office.

● Once you have decided on a theme for your role play, work with the children to consider the opportunities for reading and writing. The material that children read can be written by other children, by themselves, on posters, forms and so on.

● If appropriate, have an old telephone or mobile phone and a telephone directory for children to look up useful suppliers to 'supply' appropriate goods.

● If it's at all possible, allow access to a computer from the role-play area. The computer can be used both for word processing and for reading and recording for a variety of purposes. For example, introduce a simple spreadsheet in order to make appointments to see the vet. If the computer allows internet access, ask children to find other competitors to your business in the local area.

● Put relevant information books in the role-play area for children to use in order to find and create more appropriate props and roles to undertake.

● Give your role-play area status by asking children to feed back on their experiences and their learning.

You Can... **Set up a book quiz**

Make the most of the books in your classroom by setting up a book quiz for the children. It needn't be complex, but should encourage all children at least to look through, and at most to read, the books on your bookshelves. If the whole school, or a whole key stage, can participate together, this can become a sponsored event to raise money for new classroom books.

Thinking points

● Before you consider setting up a book quiz, it's worth thinking about all the other kinds of reading experience children are having at any one time. In order to be really valuable, the classroom book quiz shouldn't take place at the same time as other reading challenges because more children will be switched-off reading by the overload of expectation than will be switched-on by joining in a quiz.

● Consider your classroom book stock before you embark on the quiz. Are the books attractive, in good condition and well displayed? Do children have easy access to them? Are there opportunities during the school day for children to browse through the books?

● If one aim of the book quiz is to encourage children to be more aware and to read the books in the classroom then these books need to be worth reading, at an appropriate level of demand and easily available.

Tips, ideas and activities

● Book quizzes can be pitched at a level, to meet the needs of your children. The big advantage of them is that they are so versatile that you can easily make a quiz which is appropriate to different expectations: so before you begin you need to consider what the purpose is, how long you want the quiz to take and what you want the children to get out of it.

● The simplest form of book quiz is to ask children to record the names and titles of books they have read, together with a couple of sentences explaining the most interesting features of the book. You – or other children in a group, can ask each child more about one or more of the books.

● Alternatively, you can set up a more traditional quiz where, for example, you:
  ● Write a number of questions on each of a given number of books and let the children record answers on a form.
  ● Display images from pages of books and ask children to guess the book and page.
  ● Ask one question about a variety of books and let children write the book and the page.
  ● Ask one research type question and ask children to find information in more than one book, listing the book and the pages where they found the information.

● You could 'theme' book quizzes so that children can select which themes they are interested in.

● You will probably need to differentiate, unless you have a reception class, in order to enable all children to participate. Make sure, too, that you allow time in class for children to read the books before the quiz if necessary, in order not to disadvantage children whose literacy skills are less developed.

You Can... **Use your school website**

Most schools nowadays have some form of website but their usage is very different: some simply post term dates; most have some photographs of the buildings and perhaps some art work; whereas a few are truly interactive. Yours doesn't have to be a website to which schools from all over the country come to seek resources, but there is no reason why it shouldn't be accessible to children from your school to support their reading and writing development.

Thinking points

● A school website should reflect some truths about the school community and have some elements which are used by the children – even the youngest children. It's not necessary for teachers to know how to build a web page, they just need to know how to add photographs or some text. Your normal policies about children's names and photographs can be respected, but you can still put activities onto your website for children to do at home and during ICT sessions in school.

● As a school you will need to decide if each class is going to have their own interactive area, or if it will be done by key stage or if it will be on an ad hoc basis according to who puts activities on the website.

● If the activities are to be meaningful, they will need to be changed regularly and credit will have to be given to those children who participate.

Tips, ideas and activities

● Have a jokes section on the website. Ask children to type out jokes that they particularly like onto a word processor so that they can be cut and pasted onto the website.

● Encourage children to write short comments or questions raised by books they have recently enjoyed.

● Write little cryptic clues about things you have been studying in class. These don't need to mean anything to anyone outside of your class so, 'Simon told us about this on Tuesday' would be enough. Encourage children to present you with written answers to these clues.

● Sample a small area of a photograph of something in the classroom (for example, the floral fabric of a doll's dress) or school (for example a close up photograph of part of the school sign). Put it on the web, together with a limited amount of information and ask children to identify it.

● Keep a weekly diary for your class on the website. Include some questions and comments in it and wait for children's feedback.

● Start a story on the website. It could be a few sentences accompanied by two scanned in images. Ask children to suggest what happens next. You can keep on posting a couple of sentences each week, based on ideas from the children, until their interest wanes or the story comes to a natural conclusion.

● Write a research question which is relevant to topics that your children are studying or they are particularly interested in. Invite children to find out information and to present it as a word-processed file on the school network. You can then post the pertinent findings together with the names of those who did the research.

You Can... **Read together at 2.30 on Thursday**

The time and the day of the week are up to you, but having a session each week when the entire school community – including cleaners, caretakers, midday supervisors, parents, carers, teachers and children – all read, together and separately, at the same time, sends a very powerful message about reading and its value to all of your children.

Thinking points

● For all of the importance we attach to reading, we spend comparatively little time enjoying it with the children. Beyond reading before home time – and even that is threatened in many Key Stage 1 classrooms – how often do you read to and with your children? How often do you get the chance of sharing a book with a few children who are drawn together not because they are in the same guided reading group, but because they just want to share the book with you?

● Putting aside a short time every week can make a significant impact on your school's perception of itself as a reading community. If you can, encourage as many members of the school community as possible to participate. This is a powerful opportunity to value your children as readers in all their diverse ways.

Tips, ideas and activities

● The idea of 'Read together at 2.30 on Thursday' is that everyone in the school should participate in interacting with a book for half an hour every week. Ideally, this session is about reading but if, to begin with, children want to bring in comics, sticker books or puzzle books allow them to do so – at least they are using a book and making meaning from text.

● This can be an ideal opportunity to encourage your 'school-shy' parents to come into school and read alongside their children. Those who are less-confident about their own literacy can bring in books or magazines which are familiar from home. The books can be in any language; as long as they are suitable for children welcome them into school. This is a much less formal occasion than coming to listen to children reading; this is about reading with children.

● Some children may prefer to spend the time by themselves or with a friend, copying out words from their reading book or tracing the pictures; others will read to each other; others will enjoy reading with adults or older pupils. This is intentionally a session where reading and being with books is valued for its own sake.

● If you decide to have these sessions, you might want to:
  ○ Organise adults in different places around the school (particularly in the library) so that children have. opportunities to read elsewhere than in the classroom
  ○ Make sure that you have resources in terms of paper and colouring pencils so that children can draw ideas from their books.
  ○ Check that children understand expectations, including the fact that if they join a group to listen to a story they are expected to stay with the group.

● It is often more successful to have these sessions every afternoon for the first half of every term and then do something different at the same time in the next half-term.

You Can... **Get involved in the Summer Reading Challenge**

Around 97 per cent of public libraries are involved in some kind of summer reading challenge, but there's nothing to stop your school having its own reading challenge too. In essence, the challenge is simply for each child to read six books during the summer holidays. The books can be of any length, difficulty or topic appropriate to the individual child and chosen by the child.

Thinking points
- During the summer holidays, you need some well deserved rest and have earned the right to curl up with a book of your choice somewhere comfortable. However, research suggests that children's learning tends to regress during the long summer holidays, so anything that encourages them to keep practising their reading makes a lot of sense. According to the Reading Agency, 'Research shows that... [the Summer Reading Challenge]... improves children's confidence and sends them back to school fired up and ready to learn.'

- The Summer Reading Challenge runs very simply: when children return a book they have borrowed from the library, they receive a sticker; when they receive six stickers they can have a certificate or a medal.

Tips, ideas and activities
- Although libraries run the Summer Reading Challenge independently, your support and preparation can make a big difference to your children's willingness to participate.

- Are all your children members of the library? If not, why not organise a library visit? (see page 40)

- Before the summer holidays, liaise with the library about this year's theme. You can spend time towards the end of the school year introducing the theme to the children and beginning to read some books with them.

- Borrow some books from the library to share with your children.

- If you teach children who are not confident with books read some library books aloud to them. If children recognise and enjoy the book, they will be more confident to borrow it.

- If you teach older children, or those who are more confident with books, read the openings of some of the easier chapter books to your class. Discuss how the book might continue, how characters might develop, what might happen in the end. You might even generate a writing task in finishing the story. The children can then borrow the book from the library during the holidays and find out how the author chose to finish the story.

- Raise awareness of the Summer Reading Challenge through school or key stage assemblies and make it clear that the school supports the libraries' work and will help to celebrate the achievements of those who enter the challenge.

You Can... Help parents to read with their children

Are you lucky enough to work in a school where parents or carers routinely read to and with their children? Even if you only have a couple of families where parents don't read with their children it is worth considering why not. On the whole, parents want their children to succeed, so why is it so hard to ensure that all children read to their parents or carers, and are read to?

Thinking points

● Are you, or have you been, a working parent or carer with young children? If so, are/were there times when your children didn't read to you or you don't/ didn't read to them? Lack of time or energy is one barrier to persuading all parents or carers to read regularly with their children. What are the other barriers in your school community?

● In many homes, barriers are linked with a lack of understanding about how to read with a child; children not wanting to read and adults not being willing to make them; children having too many demands on their time; a lack of understanding of the language or poor adult literacy skills. These are very common, but there may well be other barriers for your parents and carers. It is important for teachers to understand the barriers to reading at home; if you don't, it becomes very hard to address the problem.

Tips, ideas and activities

● Have you got a clear idea about which children read to or with their parents and carers regularly at home? Do you know *how* these adults listen to their children read? Do you know why some children don't read at home? Is it worth doing a written survey of parents and carers to see if you can find out more about patterns of reading at home?

● If your parents or carers lack confidence in their own literacy or English language skills, why not send home some reading games to play alongside a book? It is quite easy to make reading games for many books or look in the teachers' guides which accompany your reading scheme, because games are often included in those. Try making some simple track games relating to a sequence of events from a book; lotto and memory games to practise high-frequency words; rhyming games; sentence-building activities with cut up words; picture quizzes around individual books; even simple jigsaws made by cutting a picture into 4–6 pieces for the parents or carers to supervise the child doing. The idea is just to give the adult and child the experience and confidence in learning together. Whichever games type you choose, make sure you can easily replace any pieces that are lost at home.

● If your parents are willing, but lack confidence in reading with their children, try sending home leaflets explaining how best they can support their children with reading. Some ideas are given in the photocopiable reading booklets 'Getting ready to read' and 'Becoming a reader' on pages 59–62. You can customise these with your school name and logo or use them as ideas to create your own booklets.

● If you have a large number of working parents and carers, try negotiating with them so that their children are heard reading at least three or four times a week.

You Can... Use ideas from the National Literacy Trust

Do you use information from the National Literacy Trust (NLT)? Their website at www.literacytrust.org.uk has a host of ideas, information, free leaflets and links to useful organisations whose aim is to promote literacy in schools and at home. The National Literacy Trust is an independent charity that 'changes lives through literacy'. It is also responsible for organising initiatives both in schools and in the wider community, including some for the DCSF.

Thinking points

● Children are much more likely to become readers because of their parents' or carers' reading habits and encouragement, than the work that teachers put in. Teachers are vital in teaching and nurturing the skills and interest, but parents or carers turn children into readers. That being the case, we need to help to spread the word about reading into the wider community.

● Is your school a 'Reading Connects' school? Do you run Reading Champions or the new Reading Angels model for your Key Stage 2 children? Do you use materials from the Family Reading Campaign to promote reading in your school and community? The National Literacy Trust runs all of these initiatives and many more. Their big concern is that 20 per cent of the UK adult population still struggles to read and write. If your reluctant readers have parents or carers who are in that 20 per cent, then there is a real danger that your reluctant readers will becomes part of the next generation of people who struggle to read and write.

Tips, ideas and activities

● Might your school be eligible for support through Reading is Fundamental (RIF)? This project aims to give books to children in disadvantaged areas. You have to apply to run a RIF project in your school and be committed to doing some fund-raising of your own. Within each project, a team of volunteers from the local community has to agree to select books for children to choose from and to hold some kind of event to promote the books. In addition to getting books into children's homes, this project encourages the spread of ideas about the importance of reading into the local community.

● The Family Reading Campaign offers activity cards, certificates for Reading Families, posters, ideas, activities and web links that you can use to support your own community reading drive. The activity cards are aimed at parents and carers of children at different ages and stages in reading. You can even download editable versions of the cards so that you can personalise them for your school. The originals are available in a number of languages.

● Are any of your reluctant readers interested in football? Reading the Game is an initiative run by the NLT and the Premier League to promote reading, writing and speaking and listening through the power of sport. Although most of the core activities are aimed at older children, posters showing football players reading, and talking about reading, may give that little boost of motivation.

● All of these initiatives and more can be accessed through the NLT website.

You Can... **Encourage RIBIT**

Do you RIBIT? Reading In Bed Is Terrific is a very easy initiative to promote reading at bedtime. It can be used to encourage older children (eight years plus) to read independently at bedtime, and to encourage parents and carers to read with and to younger children. You can make RIBIT more or less formal but all the feedback suggests that having prizes available makes the initiative more appealing, especially to boys.

Thinking points

● Why do many adults enjoy reading in bed – even if it's only a few pages? Anecdotal information gives answers such as it's the only point during the day when they have time to relax, that's where they're most comfortable, it's an excellent way of ridding the mind from the day's concerns, it's the easiest place to be if you want to be transported into another world…

● All of these answers would be as true for children as they are for adults. A bedtime story is still a tradition in many houses, but in others it's gradually being eroded into a story tape, CD-ROM or DVD at bedtime. Listening to story tapes has a function, but it's quite different from the experience of having a cuddle and listening to a bedtime story. If RIBIT can encourage some families to reinstate the bedtime story, then surely it's got to be a good idea!

Tips, ideas and activities

● You can run RIBIT as formally or as informally as you like. At its least structured, you simply ask parents and carers to write the date and the book title they read to their child, and once they have read a given number of books or read on a given number of occasions, they are rewarded with an agreed prize.

● A more structured version would be to give out special RIBIT cards to all participants, together with a suggested book list and book-related activities to do. Parents and carers then sign when a book has been read and the child also signs to indicate that the activities have been completed. Again, after an agreed number of books, there is a reward.

● RIBIT is an American idea, but it doesn't appear to have its own promotional mascot or character. Why not choose your school's RIBIT character based on images from commercially available stickers? That way, you can reward children's RIBIT reads with special stickers featuring the character. You may decide to give a sticker after every book read and a bigger prize after the first 50 books. Or, give a sticker after every five books and a bigger prize after 20, 50 or 100. You need to choose the appropriate number for your school.

● The best prize for reading must be a book. Explore avenues for acquiring books that won't break the literacy budget, but that will be appealing, attractive and, above all, desirable. On-line bookshops have many sales for children's books, or you may even manage to negotiate a deal in a local bookshop.

● RIBIT is easily adaptable to meet your school's needs. You need to consider:
  ○ Whether the scheme will be open to all children.
  ○ How to reward children for reading.
  ○ How to finance the rewards.

You Can... **Support the Six Book Challenge**

The Six Book Challenge is run by the Reading Agency, in partnership with the National Literacy Trust. It is aimed primarily at adults who are working to improve their own literacy levels. The challenge – which is to read six books – runs from January to May each year and is supported by libraries. The website is www.sixbookchallenge.org.uk.

Thinking points

● High levels of adult literacy make it easier for children to learn about reading in the home. Conversely, if there are low levels of adult literacy in the home, it can be very difficult for young children to understand why people would ever bother to learn to read. If their role models can't or won't read, why should the children? This not only has a knock-on effect on children's literacy, but it also impacts on home/school relationships as so much communication is by the written word.

● If we can support our children's parents and carers as they try to improve their own literacy, it will have a positive knock-on effect on the children and their attitude and attainment in reading.

● It's not your sole responsibility to spread literacy throughout the community, but often it takes one person's energies to start a scheme up before a member of the local community can be persuaded to take responsibility for continuing to run the group.

Tips, ideas and activities

● Do you know how many of your children's parents and carers struggle with literacy? How many of them would benefit from support with reading? Adults often don't want to admit to their own lack of literacy but given that the potential impact on their children is so great, it is useful if your school can establish honest and open dialogue with parents and carers about this issue. This is often easier with parents whose first language isn't English.

● The level of support you can offer to parents and carers will vary enormously depending on the support and resources already available locally, and the size of your school's budget for work within the community. But some ideas of things you can possibly do to support the Six Book Challenge are:
  ○ Set up a book group specifically for the challenge in school, either during school or after hours. It doesn't need to be run by you – it can be run by any member of the community. Some members of non-teaching staff might themselves be grateful for the opportunity to improve their reading skills.
  ○ Make space on your school library shelves for books to be borrowed by adults reading for the challenge and invest in suitable books. These can be sourced at www.firstchoicebooks.org.uk, an organisation managed by the Reading Agency, who selects and commissions books aimed at adult emergent readers.

● If you find it difficult to get fathers involved in any of your family reading initiatives, you may want to think about taking them off-site. Organising a room in your local pub or sports club for a Dads' reading group may get better results than trying to run such a group in school.

You Can... Agree targets for improvement with children

In order to move forwards, children benefit from having a clear idea about what moving forward might look like. Your reluctant readers also need to know how they stand to gain from making the effort required to make the progress. Trying to put this in language and concepts that children understand isn't always easy, but the effort is worth it if the result is that children make progress.

Thinking points

● One key issue, when thinking about targets for reluctant readers, is the question of their self-esteem. Even very young children are often aware that others can do things that they can't do. For some children – often girls – this provides an incentive to try harder; for others – often boys – this provides evidence that trying doesn't work, so you might as well not try. By the time children are in Year 2, this has often developed into an attitude towards failure: *if I try, then I might fail, but if I don't try then I can't fail.*

● Learning involves risk taking. If children are not sufficiently confident to be prepared to take risks, they are likely to grind to a halt with their learning. It is worth bearing this in mind as you negotiate targets with children, because understanding their attitude to learning will help you to agree appropriate targets.

Tips, ideas and activities

● There is a wealth of research evidence to support the fact that children are more likely to achieve targets that they have been involved in setting. This makes sense partly since if a child has decided on their target then it can be assumed that the child has some understanding of what that target might involve.

● The assessment for learning mantra is that for the learner to make progress, the teacher and learner together need to know where the learner is with their learning, agree where the learner wants to be and how they are going to bridge the gap. Since assessment for learning is now meant to drive planning forwards in the classroom, the implication is that all learners should be beginning to take some responsibility for their own learning and that responsibility involves developing an understanding of what it means to make progress.

● Reluctant readers probably need individual targets which recognise the reason that they are failing to make appropriate progress.

● You may find it easier to offer your readers a short menu of two or three targets, each of which would allow them to make progress on a different front for example, 'to learn seven more letters; to sound out three letter words; to read at least two new books each week'. The child probably needs to meet all of these targets, but offering a choice can help the child to feel that they have some involvement in their own learning. Of course, the fact that a child has only chosen one target, doesn't mean that you can't work towards more than one.

● It is useful to start the target-setting process by offering reading targets that the child is very close to achieving already. If they can tick off a target very quickly, they are likely to feel more positive towards the process of working towards targets.

You Can... **Use targets for improvement**

Once the targets are in place, how do you monitor progress towards them? If the target-setting process happens once a term and then targets are forgotten about, they are unlikely to contribute to the children's progress. On the other hand, target setting and monitoring is time-consuming. In order for it to yield results, the process needs to be streamlined and useful.

Thinking points

● How does the target-setting process happen in school at the moment? Are all children working towards the same target or differentiated targets? Or is this a process which isn't yet embedded in your school? Whatever the answer, it is likely that your reluctant readers will need their own targets.

● For most reluctant readers, there will be a number of potentially useful targets. Sometimes, the problem is deciding which to address next. As well as giving the child some choice (see page 52), make sure that it will be possible for them to achieve whichever target they select by ensuring that all the choices reflect what you are going to teach. For example, don't give options of targets relating to reading stories if you are about to teach a poetry unit.

Tips, ideas and activities

● Where will you keep children's targets? Some schools put targets on classroom walls, on flaps in the children's books, on the front of reading records, on a reading bookmark, on a laminated sheet... Wherever you choose to put them, the targets are likely to be most successful if:

- They are in sight, so the child keeps on being reminded that they exist; targets on an IEP, in a file, quickly get forgotten.
- They are continually repeated, so the child is constantly reminded what they are trying to achieve.
- They are written in child-friendly language, so the child understands what they mean.
- They are somewhere where they can easily be replaced as they are achieved. If a child has achieved a target, they need fairly immediate feedback and congratulations, quickly followed by new negotiated targets. This keeps the child focused and motivated. It may be difficult to replace targets which are laminated or displayed on walls.

● Keeping a record of targets achieved is also invaluable for your reluctant reader, because they can see how many targets they have achieved. Spending a few minutes, every now and again, reading through the list of targets achieved can make a child feel very positive about continuing to strive towards their new targets. (It's also a good record for parents or carers, the School Management Team and Ofsted.)

● For reluctant readers, try to keep to targets that can be achieved at least once within a week. You can gradually increase the length of time for working towards a target, but the more children can be seen to achieve the better for their motivation and self-confidence.

● If you need to go back and revisit a target that has already been marked as 'achieved', try to rephrase it using different words, so the child doesn't get a feeling of regression.

You Can... **Choose activities to reach your targets**

Your targets are set and the child understands what they need to do and where you are recording progress. The next stage is to think of the activities. How closely directed to the target do you want them to be? Are you going to try to focus all of your teaching towards the one target, or are you going to teach a variety of skills, including those that will help to achieve the target?

Thinking points

● You will know the children in your own class better than anyone else in school, so you will know best how to motivate them. Are literacy targets the answer for all of your reluctant readers, or might some achieve better if you give them targets around behaviours rather than specifically around reading? For example, if a child shows no interest in listening to stories, might it be appropriate to set a target around the behaviours of listening rather than around listening to stories specifically? If a child is getting bogged down in learning initial sounds, you may want to consider a target around playing general listening games, or even around listening to sounds in music lessons, rather than a target specifically identifying something that the child may resist.

Tips, ideas and activities

● Different types of targets needed to be taught differently. A target which asks that a child read a number of times a week will need different activities from a target that asks that children learn to recite the alphabet, which will in turn need different activities from a target that asks children to sound out at least the initial sound in a word when reading. When you are agreeing targets, it is worth bearing in mind how you are going to support the child in reaching them.

● Time and again, research has shown that narrowly teaching towards a specific target does not necessarily mean that the target is achieved. Children's learning tends not to be so straightforward. Narrow teaching often leads to narrow learning, where the child may appear to acquire a skill in one discreet context, but they may not be able to apply this skill to other contexts.

● Broader teaching activities, where children are encouraged to make progress in a general skills area, can be more productive since children are presented with a variety of different approaches to meeting their target. So, for example, if a child's target is to sound out initial letters when reading, any kind of activity which involves reading, hearing or recognising initial sounds, manipulating letters to spell CVC words, making sets of objects that begin with the same sound and so on will support the child in reaching the target.

● Can activities across the curriculum also be used to teach around a target? If a child feels that they have failed to acquire a certain skill, it is sometimes better to approach it obliquely, using an entirely new approach, rather than revisit something that the child already feels that they have failed at.

You Can... **Evaluate an intervention**

How do you evaluate the impact of interventions for children in your class? Any intervention is expensive, not only in cash terms but also because choosing to implement one intervention you are implicitly deciding not to try a different one which might benefit other children. It is always worth considering whether or not the intervention you chose was successful and if you would try the same thing another time or how you would vary it.

Thinking points

● 'Intervention' can mean anything from differentiated targets, to an IEP, to individual or small group work, or to implementing a published programme. For different children in different classrooms and schools, different interventions are successful. But no matter what you choose to do, doing something different is an intervention which really needs to be evaluated, however informal the process.

● Evaluating the impact of different treatments on reluctant readers is tricky because the outcome may not be measurable in terms of Early Learning Goals (ELGs) or progress towards the next National Curriculum level. The immediate impact may well be much more subtle in terms of a child's willingness to attempt something or their attitude towards learning. Nonetheless, some attempt should be made to evaluate what you did in order to inform yourself about the efficacy of an intervention.

Tips, ideas and activities

● Ask your SENCO if there are already systems in place in school for evaluating classroom interventions. If there are already policies and forms in school, you may wish to see which are most appropriate to your children.

● Considering the targets set and achieved may be sufficient. Look at targets that were achieved before the intervention and those that were achieved during it. Can you draw any conclusions about the value of the work that was done through this process?

● Depending on the level at which your children are achieving, can you make links to ELGs, P scales or National Curriculum levels? Highlighting statements about the child's attainment before you begin the intervention and repeating the process at the end of it may give you useful information.

● If your targets were focused more on self-esteem and on motivation, try asking the child questions before and after an intervention and recording the answer on a six-point scale. If you feel this is too abstract for the child, try recording your own view of the child's self-esteem, willingness to learn and motivation.

● The intervention may be successful in terms of negatives, for example: 'The target child hasn't prevented others from working, hasn't disrupted the class during story time, hasn't thrown or hidden a book bag every morning.'

● Once you have gained some idea of the impact of the intervention on the target child, briefly consider what the options would have been. Would it have been better to: postpone any intervention; persuade colleagues who take an earlier class to put interventions in place; ask a teaching assistant to work with a small group rather than putting individual pressure on an individual child or work with an individual rather than a group?

Child's profile

Child's name: Today's date:
Date of birth: Home language:
Latest hearing test – date: Result:
Latest vision test – date: Result:
Brief description of concern:

Is there any history of speech and language therapy involvement?

(Mark the following using the scale 6 = very good; I = very poor.)

— —

Can the child:

Concentrate for an age-appropriate length of time on a self-chosen activity?
6   5   4   3   2   I

Concentrate for an age-appropriate length of time on a teacher-chosen activity?
6   5   4   3   2   I

Make his/her needs understood?
6   5   4   3   2   I

Make his/her interests understood?
6   5   4   3   2   I

Sustain listening to a story with pictures?
6   5   4   3   2   I

Sustain listening to a story without pictures?
6   5   4   3   2   I

Remember an instruction with up to three commands?
6   5   4   3   2   I

On the reverse of the sheet, ask the child to draw themselves and write their name.

Phonological awareness MOT

Child's name: Date of birth: Date of MOT:

Look at the pictures. They are a cat, a hen, a tin and a sun.

Which picture:
1) starts with *c*?
2) ends with *t*?
3) I'm going to say the sounds in a word: *t-i-n*. What was the word?
4) Can you say all the sounds in this word? (Point to *hen.*)
5) Which of these pictures show the new word if I change the *p* in *pat* to *c*?
6) Which of these pictures show the new word if I change the *r* in run to *s*?
7) Which of these pictures show the new word if I change the *e* in *ten* to *i*?
8) Which of these words rhymes with *fun*: *cat, hen, zip, sun*?
9) Listen to these words: *six, sun, ten*. Which begins with a different sound?
10) Listen to these words: *hen, cat, pot*. Which ends with a different sound?
11) Which word doesn't rhyme: *dog, log, door, frog*?
12) Tell me some words that begin with *s*; that rhyme with *four*?
13) How much of the alphabet can you say?
14) Tell me the days of the week.
15) How high can you count up to?

PHOTOCOPIABLE

Behaviours associated with dyslexia

This checklist should not be used as part of a diagnosis. It may be useful, however, for recording progress or as part of a request for further assessment.

Child's name: Date of birth: Date:

Is the child:

Clumsy?	☐ Yes	☐ No
Badly organised?	☐ Yes	☐ No
Forgetful?	☐ Yes	☐ No

Does the child:

Have neat handwriting?	☐ Yes	☐ No
Confuse the order of letters in a word? Words in a sentence?	☐ Yes	☐ No
Reverse letters and numbers? Ever mirror write?	☐ Yes	☐ No
Listen and concentrate well in class?	☐ Yes	☐ No
Have difficulty pronouncing multi-syllabic words?	☐ Yes	☐ No
Find it difficult to 'find' words to say?	☐ Yes	☐ No

Can the child:

Thread beads on a lace without dropping the lace or the beads?	☐ Yes	☐ No
Tie shoelaces?	☐ Yes	☐ No
Balance on one leg for five seconds?	☐ Yes	☐ No
Sequence the days of the week?	☐ Yes	☐ No
Sequence the alphabet?	☐ Yes	☐ No
Repeat four numbers in the opposite order from the order given?	☐ Yes	☐ No
Remember and follow a sequence of three instructions?	☐ Yes	☐ No
Say if two words rhyme? And give a list of rhyming words?	☐ Yes	☐ No
Tell you the sounds at the beginning and end of words?	☐ Yes	☐ No
Copy writing accurately?	☐ Yes	☐ No

Your child is

Getting ready to read

When you have finished reading try:

- talking about the book. Ask questions like:
  - o *Did you enjoy the book?*
  - o *What was the book about?*
  - o *What was your favourite part? Why?*

Give your child the chance to talk about other books they would like to read and note them here:

Other activities you might enjoy together include:

- playing games like *Snap!* or *Lotto.*
- tracing and colouring activities.
- listening to stories read on video and audio.
- reading and talking about books together.

4

Your child is...

Getting ready to read

This means that they:

- read short books with very few words on a page.
- need to talk about a book before they try to read it.
- read using memory rather than the words.
- need to use the pictures to help them.
- are beginning to use the first sound in a word to try to see what it is.
- need to learn to recognise some of the common words like *the, my, with, here, look*.
- need to learn to recognise the names of the characters in their reading books.

2

You can help your child at home by:

- making sure that you read with them as often as possible – at least five times a week.
- making your reading time special and fun.
- talking with your child about the book before they read it.

Try asking questions like:
- o *Who is this?*
- o *What do you think they're doing?*
- o *Why do you think they're doing it?*

As you read the book with your child:
- check that they know where to start reading on the page.

If they get stuck:
- encourage them to use the picture to work out words.
- suggest that they look at the beginning sound. If they don't recognise the sound, tell them what it is.
- encourage them to guess what the word might be.
- tell them the word. Don't spend too long over each word.

3

Your child is
Becoming a reader

When you have finished reading try:

- talking about the book. Ask questions like:
  - *Did you enjoy the book?*
  - *Who was your favourite character? Why?*
  - *Why did they...?*

Give your child the chance to talk about other books they would like to read. Why not join the library?

Other activities you might enjoy together include:

- reading poetry books.
- drawing pictures about interesting events in books you read.
- playing word games like *I spy* and memory. games like *I went to market and I bought...*

4

Your child is...

Becoming a reader

This means that they:

- read short books with a few lines of text on each page.
- need to look through a book before they try to read it.
- use at least the first letter in a word and sometimes more of the letters to try to work out a word.
- use the pictures and the meaning of a sentence to work words out.
- recognise many of the most common words and need to learn some less common words like *these, people, friend.*
- are beginning to use some expression when they are reading.

You can help your child at home by:

- making sure that you read with them as often as possible – at least five times a week.
- making your reading time special and fun.

As you read the book with your child:
- o encourage them to use some expression.
- o congratulate them when they manage to work out a word.
- o make comments about what is happening in the story.

If they get stuck:
- ask what they think the word might be.
- help to sound the word out and then blend the sounds together to make the word.
- reread the sentence from the beginning for them so that they can hear the pattern of language in the sentence. This sometimes helps them to make a good guess.
- suggest that they look at the picture for clues.
- tell them the word. Don't spend too long over each word.

2

3

Index

A
active reading p22, 25
adult literacy p48, 51
anthologies p26
assessment for learning p41, 52
attention p6, 37
attitude p5
authors p33, 34, 35

B
barriers to learning p5, 31, 48
beat p28
bedtime stories p33, 50
behaviour patterns p6, 12, 58
blurbs p32
book fairs p33
books p32, 33, 43, 44
British Dyslexia Association p12

C
characters p16, 17, 18
Child's profile sheet p7, 56
comic strips p16
competition p5
compound words p9
comprehension skills p15, 21, 23
computer resources p11, 13
computer skills p19, 20, 38, 43, 45
copyright law p30
creative responses to stories p22

D
deduction p25
difficulties in reading p7
digraph recognition p9
Disability Discrimination Act (2005) p12
doodling p26
drama p19, 22
drawing p10, 15
dyslexia p12, 58

E
Early Years Foundation Stage (EYFS) p18
environmental print p10, 36
evaluating intervention p55

F
family reading initiatives p49, 51
fiction p21, 34, 40
films p18

G
games p10, 13, 14, 19, 27, 48
genre p34
grapheme recognition p12, 14

H
hearing p7, 56
high-frequency words p9, 12, 37
home reading p41, 48, 49, 51

I
illustration p10, 15, 23
illustrators p23, 33, 34, 35
inference p15, 25
information sources p20, 38
information tool kits (literacy) p37

instructions p16, 38, 39
interactive activities p17, 34, 37, 45
interest p5, 6, 15, 17
internet navigation p20
intervention p6, 55
interviews (reading habits) p41
Irlens test p12

L
language skills p6, 7, 18, 31, 56
Letters and Sounds p8, 9, 13
libraries p20, 40, 47
listening skills p6, 54

M
main idea p24
maturity p5, 6
meaning p10, 23, 25, 36
memory p8, 12, 14
monitoring progress p53
motivation p6, 15, 16, 17, 22, 53, 55
motor skills p7
multimodal learning p18, 19, 20
music p9, 14, 22, 28

N
National Literacy Trust (NLT) p5, 34, 35, 49
non-fiction p6, 15, 21, 24, 34, 40

O
on-line reference tools p20

P
parent support p19, 48
patterns p13
persuasive language p32
phonological awareness p7, 8, 9, 12, 57
pictures p15, 21
plot p18
poetry p26, 27, 28, 29
poetry awards p30
prediction p25
Primary Framework for literacy (renewed) p18
progress p53
pronunciation p9
prose p26, 29
punctuation p11
puzzle activities p14, 16, 39

Q
quizzes p34, 44

R
'Read together' sessions p46
reading aloud p19, 25, 28, 33
reading booklets p48, 59–60, 61–62
reading difficulties p7
Reading In Bed Is Terrific (RIBIT) p50
reading initiatives p46, 47, 49, 50, 51
reading interviews p41
Reading is Fundamental (RIF) p49
Reading the Game p49
reading time p22, 46
reference tools p20, 38
reluctance p6, 13, 31, 32
rhyme p8, 13, 26, 27, 29
rhythm p14, 26, 28

RIBIT (Reading In Bed Is Terrific) p50
RIF (Reading is Fundamental) p49
risk taking p52
role play p10, 19, 22, 31, 36, 43
Rose Report (2006) p8

S
school website p45
scopic sensitivity p12
self-esteem p7, 52, 55
sense and meaning p10, 11, 25, 36
sentences p11
sequencing activities p10, 12, 13, 16, 21
setting p18
shared reading p10, 11
signs p10, 36, 39
Six Book Challenge p51
sorting activities p 9, 40
sound awareness p27
speech p7, 56
spreadsheets p43
stories p16, 22, 23, 31, 45
story worlds p31
storyboards p18
Summer Reading Challenge p47
syllable structure p9, 28

T
targets p52, 53, 54
timetable displays p21
tool kits for literacy p37
treasure hunts p42
TV programmes p17

V
vision p7, 56
visiting guests p26, 35
visits p40, 47
vocabulary p42

W
website (school) p45
whole-school poetry awards p30
whole-school reading sessions p46
word processing p43, 45
word recognition p15, 23
word structure p9
writing activities p19, 23

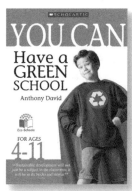

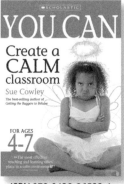

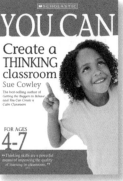